FAMOUS STORIES
OF INSPIRING HYMNS

Famous Stories
of Inspiring Hymns

ERNEST K. EMURIAN

BAKER BOOK HOUSE
Grand Rapids, Michigan

Copyright 1956
Reprinted 1975 by
Baker Book House
ISBN: 0-8010-3317-9
Library of Congress
Catalog Card No. 56-10727

PHOTOLITHOPRINTED BY CUSHING - MALLOY, INC.
ANN ARBOR, MICHIGAN, UNITED STATES OF AMERICA
1975

To

the members of

Elm Ave. Methodist Church,

Portsmouth, Virginia,

in

loving appreciation

for

nine happy years

as

their pastor

CONTENTS

ALL HAIL THE POWER OF JESUS' NAME

John Wesley was peeved because Edward Perronet, one of his young itinerant ministers, refused to preach in his presence. "It isn't that I don't want to preach, Mr. Wesley," the young preacher explained, "but that I feel so inadequate trying to proclaim the Gospel when you are in the congregation."

"Enough of that," the founder of the Methodist Church said. "I want to hear you preach as I want to hear all my preachers preach."

Perronet was twenty-three years old when he accompanied Wesley on one of his preaching tours through northern England in 1749. But he was a thorough-going Methodist in every sense of the word, having turned his back upon plans to take Holy Orders in the Church of England in order to be more closely associated with the new evangelism being proclaimed so effectively by Wesley and Whitfield. It was on this tour that Wesley sought to put the youth "on the spot." Seeing him in the congregation one night, the older man solemnly announced, "Tomorrow morning at five o'clock service, the sermon will be delivered by one of the young ministers of our connection, Edward Perronet."

The young man was visibly disturbed at being caught off guard, but he hastened to get control of himself so as to show no outward sign of his inner feelings. Anxious to avoid a scene before the people as well as a clash with his leader, he politely acknowledged the appointment and accepted the assignment. The following morning he took charge of the service, announcing the hymns, reading the Scripture lessons from both the Old and New Testaments, and delivering the prayers. When the time for the sermon arrived, the nervous minister stood up and addressed the assembled congregation. "My friends," he began, "I have been associated with Mr. Wesley for some time now, by my own choice, and not once have I refused to do anything that he asked of me. When we were staying in the same house together in Bolton, I faced an angry mob with him, suffering physical pain as well as humiliation on his behalf. On several occasions, Mr. Wesley has professed his admiration for me as a friend and co-worker, for which I am humbly grateful. But I have purposely asked him not to call upon me to preach in his presence, because I feel incapable of adequately breaking for you the bread of life when he can do it so much more effectively. As for my message to you this morning, let me merely explain that I was not consulted prior to Mr. Wesley's announcement of last night, nor had I consented to fill the pulpit this morning. Consequently I am going to deliver the finest and noblest sermon ever preached." With that, he opened the New Testament to the fifth chapter of Matthew and proceeded to read the entire Sermon On The Mount. When he finished reading the parable of the houses built on the sand and on the rock, he brought the service to a close.

After eight years of working together, their friendship began to cool, the rift becoming greater as Perronet attacked the Anglican Church with increasing fervor. After their break, he drifted from one religious group to another in search of congenial companionship, finally taking charge of a Dissenting Church at Canterbury where he spent the closing years of his life.

He was past middle age when he wrote the one hymn with which his name is now associated. A twenty-year-old organist, William Shrubsole, had composed a thrilling hymn tune he called "Miles' Lane." Augustus Toplady wanted to print the music in the November, 1779, issue of "Gospel Magazine" which he edited. When the music appeared in print, it was arranged for the first stanza of a new hymn from the pen of Edward Perronet, "All hail the power of Jesus' Name." The response of the public was enthusiastic and readers implored the editor to print the entire hymn which seemed so perfectly to express the majestic mood of the music. The April, 1780, issue of the journal carried all eight stanzas of Perronet's hymn, although there was some question as to the true identity of the author. However, on the wings of a new tune, the new stanzas were launched, quite the opposite from the usual procedure.

It was not long before the new hymn crossed the Atlantic and was heard in American Churches as often as in the British cathedrals, and it was in Boston that Oliver Holden (1765-1844) first discovered them. This versatile man was at various times a successful carpenter, composer, compiler and editor of music books, real estate operator, Congressman and Puritan preacher. But in 1792 he dashed off a thrilling hymn tune which he called "Coronation" after the last line of the poem before him, "And crown Him Lord of all." There is a tradition that the triumphant notes of his finest tune were occasioned by the birth of his first son. The organ at which he wrote his composition is now one of the proudest possessions of the Bostonian Society, and is on display in that city's famous Old South Church.

Some scholars affirm that "Coronation" is the "oldest American hymn tune in general use today," while others point out that it was originally composed in "quasi-fugue" style, with the male voices singing the lines "Bring forth the royal diadem" and the entire congregation joining in on "And crown Him Lord of all."

James Ellor, a native of Lancashire, England, composed the third tune to which this hymn is sung, "Diadem," in 1838, when he was a lad of nineteen, preparing it for a Sunday School anniversary in the local Wesleyan Church in which he held his membership. Its popularity is well deserved, as a more dramatic and dynamic musical setting would be hard to find.

The universal appeal of this famous hymn unites "every kindred, every tribe" under the banner of the Cross, through their common allegiance to Jesus Christ as Saviour and Lord.

ART THOU WEARY, ART THOU LANGUID?

It would be difficult to find two more divergent and contrasting places than a monastery in the wilderness of Judaea and a rundown old people's home in an obscure section of East Grinstead, in England. But the poems written in the monastery and translated by the warden of the almshouse, John Mason Neale, created a new era in Christian hymnody.

Following completion of studies at Cambridge in 1840, his twenty-second year, Neale was offered the poor and insignificant parish at Crawley, in Sussex. When his lungs were found to be badly affected, he had to decline the appointment, and went, instead, to Madeira for a year, in an attempt to improve his physical condition. Upon his return to England he turned down a position at Perth because the climate was too cold and damp, and accepted, as a last resort, the afore-mentioned position at East Grinstead.

Although he was a very learned man, with a mastery of at least twenty languages, and abilities beyond the ordinary, he was never appreciated by his ecclesiastical superiors. In fact, some of them treated him very unjustly. But, with unflagging zeal that belied his weak body, he toiled harder than ever to advance the revival of religion and to promote the establishment of orphanages, schools for girls, a sisterhood and a residence for the reclamation of the Magdalenes of society. This last act almost cost him his life, despite the fact that he was a man of gentle nature as well as vast learning. In 1857, while he was conducting the funeral of one of the women, some scoundrel spread the rumor that the deceased had been "decoyed into the home, persuaded to leave all her money to the sisterhood and then purposely sent to a place where scarlet fever was rampant." A mob quickly gathered and attacked the minister, threatening to take his life. However, after being roughly handled, he was permitted to return home.

As if that were not enough, his Bishop ordered him to abandon some of his social work, since several of his immediate superiors did not approve of the religious system Neale pursued. Although he died at forty-eight, Neale "lived all opposition down" before his early death, after five months of intense suffering, on August 6, 1866.

From the standpoint of the world, his life was a complete failure. But, in spite of the limitations of East Grinstead, and the struggle to exist and maintain a home for himself and his wife on his little stipend, he acquired a world-wide reputation as an industrious, thorough, and dedicated scholar as well as a voluminous writer and translator. The last half of his life was a remarkably productive period, during which he wrote numerous books of history and biography, commentaries on the Bible, and essays and articles almost without number, in addition to volume after volume of some of the most exquisite translations and original poems in the English language. It was Neale who dug up the rich hymnody of the eastern Churches, which had been buried for over a thousand years, and prepared it to minister to the Church of his own day. Since most of the devotional literature written in Greek was prose, he labored to reduce the lyrics of the ancient saints to poetry, that they might be sung, as originally intended. Selecting his own rhythm and meter, he produced gem after gem that had long been hidden beneath the dust of the centuries in a tongue that was alien to nineteenth century England.

In ancient manuscripts he became acquainted with Stephen the Sabaite (725-815 A.D.) who lived for eighty years in the Mar Saba Monastery, five hundred feet above a canyon floor in the rocky waste lands south of Jerusalem. In an old volume located in Constantinople, Neale found some of Stephen's hymns which had been born out of a spiritual pilgrimage that had ended with his whole-hearted dedication to Christ and his complete withdrawal from the world to a monastery in the custom of his day. Translating this poem freely, in the form of a dialogue between a seeker and one who has already found the an-

15

swer, he wrote the hymn which became the favorite of President Franklin D. Roosevelt:

Art thou weary? Art thou languid? Art thou sore distressed?
"Come to me," saith One, "and coming, Be at rest."

From a "Great Canon" by Andrew of Crete, he wrote "Christian, dost thou see them, On the holy ground?" And from John of Damascus, the greatest of the Mar Saba monks, he translated "The day of resurrection" and "Come ye faithful, raise the strain." "All glory, laud and honor" was inspired by a poem written about 820 A.D. by Theodulph of Orleans, while from Bernard of Cluny's "De Contemptu Mundi" he translated "Jerusalem the golden." "Christ is made the sure foundation" and "O come, O come Immanuel" were alike inspired by writings of unknown ancient Latins and translated by the almshouse warden who was more at home in the languages and culture of the early centuries than in that of his own day.

Despite the fact that most of his life was spent in ministering to women and girls, in an atmosphere that was conducive to pessimism and frustration, his hymns contain a quality of masculinity and Christian optimism rarely equalled and never surpassed.

When he found it difficult to make friends with many clergymen who occupied more exalted positions in the Church and thus were loathe to regard him as a brother minister, he made the saints of the early and medieval Church his intimate companions and, because of his fellowship with them through their writings, will be remembered and revered as long as the Church endures.

BENEATH THE CROSS OF JESUS

"Mother was a descendant of the Douglas clan, Mr. Arnot," Miss Clephane said to the editor of the popular Scottish Presbyterian magazine "Family Treasury," "and Elizabeth was proud of the Douglas blood that flowed in her veins. I can almost hear her reciting "Scots wha hae with Douglas bled" and "Douglas, Douglas, faithful and true."

"And she died here at Bridgend House?" the minister-editor asked.

"Yes," his hostess replied. "My sister passed away three years ago after a long illness, February 19, 1869, at the age of thirty-nine. When she died we felt like singing 'The Doxology,' because she had suffered a great deal."

"She must have been a remarkable woman," Mr. Arnot continued. "I wish I had had the privilege of knowing her personally."

"You would have loved her, Mr. Arnot, as everyone who knew her loved her. She was always doing things for other people. Once she even persuaded me to let her sell our horse and carriage because there were some hungry people in our neighborhood, and she felt it was wrong for us to enjoy the luxury of riding when so many people were actually starving."

"Had she been writing poetry very long?" the pastor asked.

"Our parents died when we were quite small," Miss Clephane explained, "and Elizabeth grew up a rather quiet child, shrinking from notice and absorbed in her books. She had a vivid imagination, though, and began to tell and write stories when still quite young. When she discovered that she had a talent for writing poems and verses, a whole new world opened before her, and writing became a passion with her, taking up most of her leisure hours."

"Were any of her poems or stories published?"

"Oh, no, Mr. Arnot. Most of her writing was done for her

17

own pleasure or to be read to an intimate group of friends. She never wrote anything to sell, because father and mother left us in good financial condition. She wrote for the sheer joy of creating and for the satisfaction that reading her works to sympathetic groups afforded her."

"Before I came down here, I had heard of Miss Elizabeth and her literary productions. Someone even told me that she was lovingly called 'The Sunbeam' of Melrose."

"Yes," her sister added. "She loved people and people loved her in turn. Despite her frail body, when she walked into a room it was almost as if someone had entered a dark cave with a lighted candle, and when she left, we felt as if someone had blown out the only light we had."

"What a beautiful tribute for a sister to pay a sister," Mr. Arnot said. "But, getting back to the purpose of my visit, you know, Miss Clephane, as editor of 'Family Treasury' I am always on the lookout for a new writer who has something to say and the gift of saying it, whether in prose or poetry. If you have any of your sister's writings, I would be grateful for the privilege of examining them. Possibly, with your permission, I can use some of them in the columns of my magazine."

Miss Clephane excused herself and left the room, returning shortly with a scrap book, which she handed to her guest. "Elizabeth kept most of her poems in this book," she explained.

Mr. Arnot opened the pages carefully, and began browsing through them, reading bits of poetry written down here and there in a clear and careful hand. Finding one gem of unusual beauty he said, "This is remarkable, Miss Clephane."

"Which one is that?" she asked.

Her guest read:

Beneath the cross of Jesus, I fain would take my stand,
The shadow of a mighty rock Within a weary land.
A home within the wilderness, A rest upon the way
From the burning of the noon-tide heat, And the burden of
     the day.

"How well I remember when Elizabeth wrote those lines. Mr. Arnot. She and I had been making a study of the life and ministry of Augustus Toplady, the man who wrote 'Rock Of Ages.'

She became interested in the use of the word 'rock' as a figure of speech in the Bible, and wrote her poem as a result of her study."

"When was that?"

"The summer before she died," his hostess replied. "The summer of 1868."

"May I make a copy of it and use it?"

"Of course, Mr. Arnot. I only wish Elizabeth were here to grant you permission with her own lips. She would have been overjoyed at the knowledge that someone wanted to share her poems with other Christian people in her beloved Scotland."

When Rev. Mr. Arnot published the four stanzas of "Beneath the cross of Jesus" in an 1872 edition of "Family Treasury," he printed the poem under the caption, "Breathings from the Border," and prefaced it with these words, "These lines express the experiences, the hopes, and the longings of a young Christian lately released. Written on the very edge of this life, with the better land fully in the view of faith, they seem to us footsteps printed on the sands of time, where these sands touch the ocean of eternity."

During the next two years, he printed several more of Elizabeth Cecelia Clephane's remarkable poems, which, but for his interest, would have been lost to the world. It was on page 595 of one of the issues published early in 1874 that he printed a poem from her pen that was to become the most effective gospel song of that century. Visiting in the Clephane home again that spring, he discovered the five stanzas of an unusual poem. "How did she happen to write these lines?" he asked her sister.

She explained, "She wrote them originally at the request of one of the Sunday School teachers in our Church. The teacher had a large class of boys and thought it would keep them quiet as well as arouse their interest if she read them a poem written by a member of the Church whom they all knew. Elizabeth had been brooding for several months over the hasty departure of our only brother. He had caused us much heartache before he finally packed up and left for Canada. Before he left home for the last time, he said rather jokingly, 'Well, you won't be able to rescue the lost sheep this time, girls, because he's going too far from the fold. Even the shepherd won't be able to locate him.' We learned later that he had actually gone to Canada, but we never saw him again. With him as well as the class of boys in mind, she wrote her poetic version of Jesus' famous parable, entitling the poem 'The Ninety and Nine.' "

From Mr. Arnot's journal the poem found its way into other magazines and papers until the memorable day, later that same year, when Ira D. Sankey discovered it in a penny newspaper in Glasgow, set it to music spontaneously in Edinburgh, and gave the world one of its most inspiring gospel songs. In the words of Mr. Arnot, "These footprints of one whom the Good Shepherd led through the wilderness into rest, may, with God's blessing, contribute to comfort and direct succeeding pilgrims." That her two hymns have done just that is the unanimous opinion of Christian people the world over.

BRIGHTEN THE CORNER WHERE YOU ARE

Sorrow and sadness inspire about as many hymns and songs as joy and gladness. It was out of her heart-break at the death of her fiance the day before their scheduled wedding that Anne Steele, the first modern woman hymn-writer, penned her hymn, "Father, whate'er of earthly bliss." Likewise, the drowning of his sweetheart on the eve of their wedding day led Joseph Scriven of Dublin Ireland to embark on the long trek that ended on the shores of beautiful Rice Lake in Ontario, Canada, where he had a religious awakening and wrote his one famous hymn, "What a friend we have in Jesus."

When doubt and despair gave way to hope and faith, twenty-two-year-old Ray Palmer recorded his spiritual autobiography in the four stanzas of "My faith looks up to Thee." And Henry Francis Lyte, who fought his way from a self-centered to a Christ-centered ministry, told the tale of his struggle in "Jesus, I my cross have taken," just as George Matheson, years later, conquered blindness and disappointment in love to become immortal through his hymn, "O love that wilt not let me go."

Elizabeth Payson Prentiss, grief-stricken when her children died in an epidemic in New York City, prayed her way through from darkness to light and left as her legacy a hymn of personal devotion, "More love to Thee, O Christ."

A similar spirit was shown by Mrs. W. S. Martin when she, with her husband and small son, was visiting friends in New York state. Her minister husband had been invited to preach in a local Church on Sunday morning and had accepted the invitation. Mrs. Martin, though, had not been well for some time, and early that Sunday took a turn for the worse. Her husband was about to pick up the telephone to ask to be relieved of his preaching engagement, when their son said, "Father, if God wants you to preach, won't He take care of mother while you are away?" The preacher hastened to the Church to deliver his message. When he returned home, his son met him, and showed him a piece of paper on which Mrs. Martin, despite her illness, had written the words of the gospel song, "God will take care of you." Later that afternoon, Mr. Martin composed the music to which her stanzas are sung, singing to her as she listened from her sick bed.

Another noble Christian woman who conquered personal disappointment in a similar way was Mrs. Ina Duley Ogdon. Friends had prophesied a glowing future for the attractive, talented young lady and she had already enjoyed the plaudits of many local congregations. "She has a great future," her neighbors said. "With her voice and her personality, she'll go a long way." And from where she stood the road loomed bright and beautiful before her.

But hardly had she embarked on her musical career when word was flashed, "Father is ill. Please come home." Sacrificing her own desire to pursue a career on the stage, she went back home to look after her invalid father. During the months that followed, she tried to ease her own heartache by making the home as cheerful as possible. "I wanted to do some deeds of greatness," she often said, "and longed to shed my light afar. But God knew best. He put me right back here and commanded me to let my light shine before my own household that they may see my good works and glorify Him who is in heaven."

In the next few years she inspired many others to look for the sun shining just behind the clouded skies, and encouraged them to use their talents for God's glory, even if their songs of cheer fell into but one heart alone. "You must reflect the Bright and Morning Star right where you are," she reminded them over and over again.

It was in 1913, the year that Rev. George Bennard wrote "The Old Rugged Cross," that Mrs. Ogdon put her Christian philosophy into poetic form, writing three stanzas of a gospel song which she entitled, "Brighten the corner where you are." After Charles Gabriel, composer of "The Awakening Chorus" as well as hundreds of other sacred tunes, set this new poem to music, Homer Rodeheaver sang it for the first time in public at a great meeting in Syracuse, New York, and sent it winging its way around the world.

Three years later, when her brother lay near death in a hospital in Chicago, she "bore her burden" nobly and well, and helped many others who were to pass through similar valleys by writing "Carry your cross with a smile."

In all, she must have written several thousand hymns, songs and religious poems, every one of them springing out of her own experience. Titles that bear her name include "God is everywhere," "Lighten the burden for someone," "My Lord abides," "When you know Jesus, too," "Jesus wants to help you," "Jesus will," and "You must open the door." Each one breathes a note of dependence upon God blended with a spirit of Christian optimism for the future with His companionship and help.

In her own life, she brightened many a corner, and, by means of her most popular sacred song, influenced more people than she could possibly have reached had she been permitted to follow a successful stage career.

CHILDREN OF THE HEAVENLY KING

"Let's sing!" John Cennick called to his brother preacher, Howell Harris, as the angry mob gathered more threateningly about them.

Harris shouted back, "If I had known that the people at Swindon were going to treat us like this—"

Cennick silenced him with a gesture and began to sing a familiar Wesleyan hymn with all the voice and enthusiasm he could muster. When he joined the Methodist movement in 1739, he didn't know what he was getting in for either. But he recalled the advice of John Wesley himself, "Always look a mob in the face," so he fixed his eyes upon the self-appointed leader of the ruffians as he sang with might and main. The gang leader was undeterred, however, and ordered some of his men to fire a shot over the heads of the two itinerant Methodists, while others began to play a fire-hose upon them. The meaner men pelted them with hogwash and beer-barrel grounds as well as with muddy water from a nearby ditch. But the two preachers sang on like Paul and Silas sang in the dark, dank dungeon at Philippi centuries earlier.

Seeing that they could not be silenced by those dirty tactics, the scoundrels hurled stones, eggs and baskets of dust and soot on the two men. But, instead of throwing them off their feet, it only drove them to their knees, where they prayed more fervently for their enemies and oppressors. "The power of Satan and the power of God are at work," Cennick cried to Harris, "and the power of God must prevail."

Then, turning to one of the mob, Cennick said, "What harm do we do? Why are you so furious against us? We only come to tell you that Christ loved you and died for you." With that, the man hurled a bucket of water in the preacher's face. Undaunted, Cennick said to him, "My dear man, if God should so pour out His wrath upon you, what would become of you? Yet I tell you that Christ loves you." With that, his adversary dropped the empty bucket, and, as his countenance paled, he shook the minister's hand and departed, under strong conviction of his sins.

Cennick was a twenty-one year old land surveyor in Reading, England, when John Wesley first met him. The founder of Methodism entered this record in his journal, "On Friday, March 1739, I came to Reading, where I found a young man who had in some measure known the powers of the world to come. I spent the evening with him and a few of his serious friends, and it pleased God to strengthen and comfort them." That young man was John Cennick. The next year, Wesley appointed the young convert to teach in a school for miner's children at Kingswood and ordained him as a lay preacher. Charles Wesley was as enthusiastic about Cennick as his brother, John, both being conscious of the gifts with which God had endowed him. But George Whitfield came on the scene shortly thereafter, and while he and the Wesleys labored jointly with great success, Cennick was swept off his feet by the emotional impact of Whitfield's pulpit oratory. Soon disagreeing with the Methodists on the interpretation of the Arminian doctrine of "Free Grace" (of which he himself had been a recipient), he left John and Charles and followed George.

Unfortunately, each man had to defend himself in this instance, and when Cennick said, "It was like being in the midst of a plague to be associated with the Wesleys," Charles referred, in like manner, to the young tutor as "that weak man, who holds to such strange doctrines." Torn between asceticism on one hand and religious fanaticism on the other, Cennick had forsaken his Quaker forbears when he joined up with Wesley. Now having forsworn him for Whitfield, it was inevitable that he leave Whitfield eventually, which he did in 1745, associating himself thereafter with the Moravians. In that move, he became a closer spiritual brother of John Wesley, since the Moravian leader, Peter Bohler, had played such a vital role in John's religious growth and development. This group rejoiced that so talented a man sought membership in their ranks and ordained him a deacon in London in 1749, little dreaming that the man whom some dubbed "a chameleon Christian" had but six more years to live.

Being thoroughly English, this native of Berkshire appreciated the wisdom of John Wesley when the latter ordered some tea pots made for the Methodists, and expressed his desire to have some brief prayers imprinted on them. "In that way," he explained to Cennick, "our people will always have a prayer to offer when they have their tea, at any hour of the day or night." Cennick rose to the occasion and gave Wesley two four-line "table graces" which later were used wherever and whenever the Methodist people paused for their "spot of tea." Written in long meter (L.M., four lines with eight syllables in each line) these "Blessings" could be sung as well as spoken. The most familiar tune to which they were sung was that which some call "The Doxology" although, technically, the name of the tune is "Old 100th," since it was the old tune to which the metrical version of Psalm 100 was sung. The favorite one was this:

Be present at our table, Lord; Be here and everywhere adored;
Thy creatures bless, and grant that we May feast in paradise
    with thee.

And the other went as follows:

We thank Thee, Lord, for this our food, But more because of
    Jesus' blood;
Let manna to our souls be given, The bread of life sent down
    from heaven.

While Cennick is said to have literally worked himself to death, what with preaching six times a day and enduring physical persecution, he took the time to write more than five hundred hymns during the four fruitful years of his ministry with Harris and Whitfield. Of these, "Jesus my All to heaven is gone," published in Bristol in 1743, and "Children of the heavenly king," printed the previous year in the author's book, "Sacred Hymns for the Children of God in the Days of their Pilgrimage," and his two "Graces" remain after the passing of more than two centuries.

It was in the spirit of his most popular hymn that Cennick lived, loved and labored during his brief life of only thirty-seven years. In the words of this poem, he fastened his eyes upon God and his heart upon his heavenly home. Obediently he marched on, through trials and tribulations as well as through days of prominence and popularity, singing the songs of Zion and following his Lord and Master, Jesus Christ. And, if he was somewhat vacillating in his earthly loyalties, there was never any doubt about the sincerity of his spiritual allegiance and the constancy of his Christian convictions.

CHRIST FOR THE WORLD WE SING

"Who makes up those slogans anyway?" one of the young men asked, as a group attending the Ohio State Convention of the Y.M.C.A. in Cleveland during February, 1869, strolled through a nearby park following the evening program.

"The committee in charge, I think," another replied. "Why?"

The first youth explained, "That one in the auditorium to-night was a good one, and I was just wondering who thought it up."

Rev. Samuel Wolcott, a fifty-six-year-old Congregational minister who was walking with the group repeated the slogan, " 'Christ for the world and the world for Christ.' That's almost better than the one they usually use, 'To know Him and to make Him known' or another one that used to be popular at these conventions 'My best for His highest' or something like that. But I like this one. It has a challenge to it that makes it appealing."

"I still want to know who thought it up," the first youth insisted.

"Maybe the grandson of the man who invented 'Remember the Alamo,' " another replied, "or a cousin of the politician who went to the White House on 'Tippecanoe and Tyler too.' "

"Or 'Fifty-four-forty or fight!' When did that come in?" another delegate asked.

An older man replied, "It had something to do with the boundary line between the United States and Canada, but the dispute was settled peaceably and no one had to fight anyone else over it, thank goodness," he concluded.

Several of the delegates sat down in some of the park benches while some of the others continued to stand around in smaller groups discussing the program and the convention in general. One of the young men turned to Dr. Wolcott and asked, "Do you think the people of the world want Christ as much as we think they ought to?"

The minister thought for a moment and then replied, "God sent Christ because He knew we needed Him, whether we knew it or not. It is that same motive that makes others go out to carry the good news to the far corners of the world. We go because we know they need Him, whether they realize it or not."

"You were a missionary once, weren't you?" another asked.

"Yes," the pastor explained. "After I was ordained as a minister in 1839, I answered the missionary call and was sent to the city of Beirut in Syria, in April of 1840, a young and inexperienced minister of twenty-seven."

"What did you do there, Dr. Wolcott?" another asked.

"I helped in a missionary school in Abieh, on Mount Lebanon, but some of the ignorant mountaineers rose up in rebellion against their ruler, the Pasha, a very wicked man, and we had to leave and return to Beirut."

"Was your school destroyed?"

"No, but in the spring of 1841 I was sent to Damascus to open a new school for the Druses. Another civil war broke out and we were dislodged for the second time. These continued hostilities among the various tribes made it impossible for me to continue my educational and evangelistic work. Since my home had been broken up by sickness and death, I left Beirut on January 2, 1843, and returned to America."

"Did you come back by the Atlantic or the Pacific?" a friend asked.

"I didn't have enough money to come back the long way, so I hurried back as rapidly as I could by way of England and the Atlantic, landing in Boston on April 21, 1843, after an absence of four years."

"Would you return if you could?"

"Yes, I would, if my health permitted, because I believe Jesus meant what He said in the great commission," the missionary replied. "My job now is to see that our Churches continue to send out their finest and best equipped young men and women to do the job some of us older men began, and to insist that the Churches continue to back them up with sufficient money to enable them to do their jobs thoroughly and effectively. My Church here in Cleveland is already undertaking the support of several missionary couples."

"Getting back to the meeting tonight, what was your impression of the speaker, Dr. Wolcott?" another delegate standing nearby asked.

"I thought he was very inspiring. The hymns were well chosen, too, I thought. We sang 'The morning light is breaking,' and 'From Greenland's icy mountains,' both written by young enthusiastic ministers. I wish they could have heard the delegates fill that vast auditorium with their music."

"The slogan would make a good hymn, wouldn't it, Doctor?" another asked.

"I hadn't thought of that," the minister answered. "But it would, wouldn't it? 'Christ for the world and the world for Christ.' That would make an excellent hymn. The slogan looked so impressive outlined in evergreens over top of the platform. Someone ought to make a hymn out of it at that, young man."

"Have you written hymns?" he was asked.

"Just once," Wolcott replied. "My friend, Rev. Darius E. Jones, asked me to write one for a new hymnal last year. I worked over it for a long time, outlining it as I do my sermons, and finally came up with 'Father, I own Thy voice.' To my amazement, Jones composed a tune for it and published it in his book 'Songs for the new life,' printed in Chicago last month."

"Then you're the man to write 'Christ for the world and the world for Christ,' " another delegate insisted.

The older man shook his head. "No," he said, "there must be others who can do a better job of it than I. I wouldn't know where to start except to say 'Christ for the world we sing.' "

"There's nothing wrong with that," another added. "It sounds like 'Come thou Almighty King.' "

Wolcott smiled. "You may have something there, young man. We can write our hymn in the same meter as 'Come thou Almighty King' so it can be sung to that same familiar tune." Before he knew it, Samuel Wolcott, who had never written so much as a poem prior to his fifty-sixth birthday, was writing

'Christ for the world we sing' with a spontaneity that surprised him and amazed those who stood around taking down the lines and phrases as they were formed in his mind and heart. When he had finished the four stanzas, he said, "Quite a contrast to the labor and toil I spent on 'Father, I own Thy voice.' This thing literally rolled out without too much conscious effort."

Before his death in Longmeadow, Massachusetts, seventeen years later, February 24, 1886, at the age of seventy-three, Wolcott had written more than two hundred hymns, and served with distinction as Secretary of the Ohio Home Missionary Society.

Whereas Reginald Heber wrote "From Greenland's icy mountains" *before* he was called to serve his Lord as a missionary Bishop in India, Samuel Wolcott wrote his finest hymn *after* serving as a faithful missionary for several years, thus earning the honor of being the only missionary ever to write an effective missionary hymn, one that has been accepted by Christendom as worthy of a permanent place in its hymnody.

COME, O THOU TRAVELLER UNKNOWN

When Thomas Koschat discovered the poem about unrequited love which began, "Forgotten, forgotten, forgotten am I," he was so moved by the sentiments that he immediately sat down and set the story to music. He little dreamed that the editor of a Christian hymnal would one day include his music in a new volume, with the stanzas of James Montgomery's great hymn on the Twenty-third Psalm, "The Lord is my shepherd, No want shall I know."

Nor did George Webb imagine that a somewhat similar experience would be his when, for an evening of entertainment aboard a passenger vessel in mid-Atlantic, he composed a new tune for the poem, " 'Tis dawn, the lark is singing." It was left to another editor to take that tune and match it with George Duffield's words and thus create one of the most militant hymns in all Christendom, "Stand up, stand up for Jesus!"

This thing also works in reverse, because it was to the tune of an old hymn written during the middle of the nineteenth century by Abbey Hutchinson, "Kind words can never die," that the British Tommies, during the First World War, sang a song of their own, substituting "Old Soldiers" for "Kind Words," giving the world the song now popular with veterans in every branch of the military, "Old soldiers never die."

Felix Mendelssohn was asked to compose a tune for a celebration in connection with an anniversary of the invention of printing. Little did he know that his music would be immortalized by being linked with Charles Wesley's superb Christmas hymn, "Hark! the herald angels sing." Nor did William Shield, who composed the tune now known as "Auld Lang Syne" for his opera "Rosina" in 1782, ever dream that his music would be the inspiration of a noble hymn of immortality, "It singeth low in every heart," which Rev. John Chadwick wrote in 1876.

Stranger still is the fact that the tune William Steffe wrote in the middle 1800s for his own gospel song, "Say, brothers, will you meet us On Canaan's happy shore," soon became associated with an entirely different kind of song, "John Brown's body lies a-mouldering in the grave." Later it was rescued from oblivion when Julia Ward Howe, while visiting at Munson Hill Farm, near Washington, D.C., was inspired to write her own hymn, "The Battle Hymn of the Republic."

But, getting back to Scotch melodies, Robert Burns came across a delightful, lilting tune one day which was called "the Caledonian Hunts' Delight" and was so intrigued by it that he sat down and wrote a poem to be sung to the tune, beginning with the line, "Ye Banks and Braes of Bonnie Doon." He learned, after he had written his poem, that the music had come about as the result of a conversation between James Miller and a Mr. Clarke some years earlier. It seems that Miller had said to his friend, "I am anxious to compose a Scots air. In fact, it has become one of the ardent desires of my heart. How do I go about it?"

Clarke, thinking Miller was joking, humorously replied, "Write your melody on the black keys of the harpsichord to a good steady kind of rhythm and you'll have what you want."

Miller, taking his friend's words as sound musical advice, and following them infallibly, did exactly that and produced the rudiments of what, with some alterations and corrections by Clarke, became the afore-mentioned tune. Burns was doubly anxious to authenticate the tune's origin since its popularity had led to the claim that it was of Irish origin.

The night Charles Wesley preached in Kingswood, May 24, 1741, he wrote these words in his diary, "I preached on Jacob wrestling for the blessing." Doubtless, the music to which Burns referred was the farthest thing from the Methodist preacher's mind as he delivered the sermon that evening. The thoughts he shared with his people that night were finally reduced to poetic form the following year, when he wrote the fourteen stanzas of one of his most profound poems, sometimes called "Wrestling Jacob," but known by its first line, "Come, O thou traveller unknown."

Meanwhile Burns' poem had become so popular that the tune to which the verses were sung was no longer known by its original title, but was called "Bonnie Doon" after the last two words of the first line of his stanzas. The name of the person who discovered that Wesley's words could be sung to "Bonnie Doon" is not known, but whoever he was, he must have made a good job of it. Because, the young lad who was to grow up to become Methodist Bishop Warren A. Candler, founder of the famous Emory University, learned the words to that tune and never forgot either one. Older hymnals carry this notation above the hymn, "Bonnie Doon, as sung by Bishop Warren A. Candler." Later the name of the tune was again forgotten, and "Wrestling Jacob" was sung to a tune now named for the Methodist leader himself, "Candler," which was nothing but "Bonnie Doon," which was originally "The Caledonian Hunts' Delight."

So a poem by an English divine, sung to a tune by a Scottish composer, popularized by a Bishop of the former Southern Methodist Episcopal Church in the United States, has won the universal acclaim it so well deserves. And "Wrestling Jacob" will be a permanent part of Methodist hymnody as long as that hymnody endures.

COME YE DISCONSOLATE

"How long do you expect to stay in the States, Mr. Moore?" Mr. Happer asked his house guest, Thomas Moore.

"Not too long, Mr. Happer," the talented young Irishman replied. "But if there are many more places like your Ballyhack Plantation, I'm liable to stay longer than I expected. I'm really a writer by trade and the quicker I get back to my pen and paper, the better."

"What were you doing in Bermuda? Getting material for a new book?" his host asked.

"Oh, no," the genial youth answered. "Last year I was offered the position as Admiralty Registrar for Bermuda by the British government. It was too good a thing to turn down so I accepted. However, I'm not much of a business man, and the duties of the office became monotonous and very boring. A few months ago I turned them over to my deputy, and set out to see the world, and so far, so good."

The Happers were honored when Moore accepted their invitation to visit their home, located on the edge of Dismal Swamp, a few miles from Norfolk, Virginia. He had already made quite a name for himself in his twenty-four years, and his fame preceded him to the southern plantation. His great charm as well as his musical ability attracted many people to him and wherever he went, he made friends easily. During his stay in Virginia he heard some of the legends about Dismal Swamp and was especially intrigued by the story of a young man who lost his mind when his sweetheart died. The distraught youth suddenly disappeared from home and was never seen or heard from again. Neighbours claimed that he fled into the fast dark recesses of the swamp, near Lake Drummond, crying out in his madness that his lover was not dead but only lost in the dreadful morass and waiting for him to find her. The gifted poet needed no more inspiration than that, and soon wrote a ballad entitled "The Lake in the Dismal Swamp."

As for his opinion of The Old Dominion, it can be found in a letter he wrote the summer of that same year, 1803, in which he said, "The characteristics of Virginia in general are not such as can delight either the politician or the moralist, and at Norfolk they are exhibited in their least attractive form." Despite his adverse impressions, the citizens of Norfolk welcomed him to their homes and showered him with attentions. Years later they spoke of him as "the homesick, lovesick Irish poet," who "sang his love songs for Virginia's belles."

After travelling extensively through the United States and Canada, Moore returned to England in 1804, to learn that his deputy in Bermuda had run away with the proceeds of a ship's cargo and that he, Moore, was being held responsible for the loss which was in excess of $30,000. With the aid of wealthy friends he managed to clear his name but he had to stay far away from Paris and London until the debt was paid in full. During these eventful years he continued to work on all kinds of books, writing novels, history, biography, religious treatises, poetry, song books and miscellaneous collections of literary odds and ends. Nominally a Roman Catholic, some of his writings breathe a religious flavor while others reveal the underlying convictions of the author in more subtle ways. He is said to have been paid $15,000 as an advance for one of his finest long poems, "Lalla Rookh," even before it was printed. The accounts of his duels and near-duels show him to be about as hot-blooded as the average Irishman of his time and age.

It was in 1816, however, that he gathered together thirty-two poems which he had written to be sung to popular airs, and published them under the title "Sacred Songs." Those who remember Moore only as the talented author of "The last rose of summer," "The harp that once through Tara's halls," "Oft in the stilly night," and the hauntingly beautiful "Believe me if all those endearing young charms," rumored to have been written to comfort his wife when she was suffering from the ravages of small pox, are surprised to know that, in this slender little book of sacred songs, there was one poem which was destined to find a permanent place in Christian hymnody. It was a lyric of three four-line stanzas, which began:

> Come, ye disconsolate, where'er ye languish,
> Come, at the shrine of God, fervently kneel.

Moore confessed that he wrote the lines to be sung to a German air to which he had taken a fancy. It is to that very tune, now named "Consolation," by Samuel Webb, that his hymn is sung universally today. The words were altered by Dr. Thomas Hastings to give the hymn an evangelical emphasis for Protestants, and the first two lines now read:

> Come, ye disconsolate, where'er ye languish,
> Come to the mercy seat, fervently kneel.

Later someone else altered the second stanza of Roman Catholic priest Frederick Faber's hymn, "Faith of our fathers, Mary's prayers Shall win all nations unto thee," to read, "Faith of our fathers, we will strive To win all nations unto thee," to make the splendid hymn acceptable to Protestants. As revised, Moore's hymn was first published sixteen years later, in 1832, and from Hastings and Mason's book, "Spiritual Songs" passed into the hymnals of the Church universal.

Unfortunately, the poet's last years were fraught with nervous tension and fits of insanity, brought about by the loss of several children to whom he was deeply devoted. His wife cared for him tenderly and lovingly until his death, at the age of seventy-five, in 1852.

His one enduring hymn should serve as a common bond between Catholic and Protestant, since it is an invitation to both to seek solace and find strength through a deeper faith in the God who loves them both equally and alike.

COME, YE THANKFUL PEOPLE, COME

When someone asked the question, "What is the penalty for bigamy?" a wag with rare insight replied, "Two mothers-in-law." Another added, "If having two wives is bigamy, then having one wife must be monotony!" While the relative merits of polygamy and bigamy are fit subjects for ethnologists and debaters, suffice it to say that there was but one, and only one, famous hymn writer who had more than the usual allotment of wives and spouses. Not that he was a bigamist or polygamist. In the words of the centenarian who boasted on his one-hundredth birthday that he had no enemies, the truth of the matter was, he just outlived them!

Such was the case with much-married George Job Elvey (1816-1893). The Scriptural Job had three daughters and suffered untold physical and mental hardships, but since this distinguished organist and composer was named at baptism, shortly after his birth, his middle name has no connection whatsoever with the fact that he outlived three wives only to be finally outlived by his fourth and last.

When a mere youth of nineteen, he won the coveted position of organist at St. George's Chapel, Windsor, over a field of competitors that included twenty-five-year-old Samuel Sebastian Wesley, whose hymn tune "Aurelia" is sung universally to Samuel J. Stone's poem "The Church's One Foundation" (although originally composed for an entirely different poem). Maybe the committee in charge heard that Wesley was more interested in piscatorial pursuits than organ playing, since the equally distinguished musician had, on one occasion, sent his assistant ahead to begin a scheduled recital while he, the maestro, tried his hand at casting in what looked like a well-stocked stream a short distance from the Church! What with four wives and a position of responsibility to hold down, Elvey had little time for such recreational sport, but filled his position with distinction for a period of forty-seven years. He was honored with a Doctorate from Oxford during his fifty-sixth year, an honor many an organist coveted but few merited.

The records show that during his first marriage, which lasted from 1839 until 1851, he devoted most of his time and talent to providing music for the royal family, having very little of either left for composing. It was during his second marriage which took place three years after his first wife's death, and lasted from 1854 until 1863, that his flair for composition began to be expressed, and from that era in his life came his noblest hymn tune, which he named for his post, "St. George's, Windsor." Originally composed for James Montgomery's hymn, "Hark, the sound of Jubilee," and published initially in 1858, it is now associated almost entirely with the thrilling hymn of thanksgiving which Rev. Henry Alford wrote in 1844, "Come, ye thankful people, come."

In 1862, during the interregnum between the passing of his second wife, who was a Miss Nichols prior to her marriage and with whom he lived nine happy years, and his discovery of Miss Elenora Jarvis, his third bride, he composed another tune, "St. Crispin." Though found in several hymnals, it sounds too much like Henry Baker's tune "Hesperus," composed in 1857, and cannot match the fervor and spirit of his first hymn tune. However, it was during his third marriage, 1865-1879, the longest of the four, that he was knighted and became Sir George for the balance of his fruitful and romantic life.

He became famous as a remarkable composer of wedding music for members of the royal family, doubtless inspired in no small degree by his own nuptial experiences and adventures. But such social events, as well as state functions, called from his fertile pen no less than two oratorios, many odes and anthems, countless chants and hymntunes, to say nothing of a tremendous volume of secular music. It was also during this marriage that he gave the world his second finest hymn tune, "Diademeta," composed for Matthew Bridges' hymn, "Crown him with many crowns." To attempt to remember that his noblest hymn tune was composed during his second marriage and his second best during his third can try the keenest memory. But his third and least-familiar tune, "Illuminatio," came from his pen during his fourth and final voyage on the sea of matrimony. He was united in wedlock this time to a sister of the ex-Lord Mayor of London in June (of all months) 1882. This relationship terminated with the groom's death in 1893, although his wife lived thirty years longer. While composed for "Rock of Ages," it is never likely to supplant the familiar tune used throughout the world, "Toplady."

It is to the credit of his fourth wife that, the year after her famous husband's death, she gathered together what data she could find about his long and interesting life and published "The life and reminiscences of Sir George Elvey." Sir George must have known that there were many bachelor hymn writers and composers as well as very many single women who added richly to Christian hymnody as both authors and composers, to say nothing of the widows and widowers who also contributed their share. But he took to heart the Scriptural injunction, "It is not good for man to be alone," and, although it was not originally written primarily to be applied to him alone, nevertheless, he obeyed it to the letter, which accounted in no small measure for the unusual and creative life that he led and the work which he was inspired to produce. The question the Sadduccees asked Jesus about the woman who had married seven brothers here on earth, "In heaven whose wife will she be?" could well be asked in reverse about this versatile man, Sir George, and his many marriages, "In heaven, whose husband will he be?"

Fortunately, answers to such queries can be safely left in the hands of the Almighty!

FLING OUT THE BANNER!

"Look, Dad, there's a church floating down the river!" sixteen-year-old William Croswell Doane shouted to his father, Bishop George Washington Doane, late one afternoon in December, 1848.

"A what?" his father asked, as he rose from his desk to join his son at the window.

"A church floating down the river," the boy replied.

William's older brother, George, rushed in from the living room to join his brother and father at the window. "What was that you said, William? It sounded like 'a church floating down the river.'"

"That's what I said, George," the younger boy explained. Then, pointing out the window of their home, "Riverside," on the campus of St. Mary's Hall, a school for girls on the Delaware River, in Burlington, New Jersey, he added, "See for yourself!"

The three stared out the window as William proudly said, "Look! What did I tell you? It's a church, isn't it?"

His father shook his head. "In all my eleven years at St. Mary's, I have never seen anything like it. It can't be a hallucination, because two of us are seeing the same thing."

"Make it three, Dad, because I can see it, too," added George. "If it's a mirage, then we're all crazy!"

"You see mirages on deserts, George, and the Delaware River is no desert. So if that thing out there isn't real, we're all batty," William commented.

Bishop Doane, named for the Father of his country, having been born in 1799, the year George Washington died, spoke up. "Whatever it is, it must be a church, because it has a church steeple on it. I'm certain of that."

"Isn't that a boat up front pulling the church?" George asked, straining to see what was actually going on out on the river.

"Yes," his father replied. "And the boat is pulling the church down the river toward Philadelphia. They must have moved an abandoned church building on to that big barge somewhere up the river."

"But who would go to church out there?" asked William. "Fishermen?"

"Don't be silly, William," George interrupted.

"Well," William protested, "why not? They have to go to church somewhere, don't they?"

Bishop Doane laughed and then said, "I remember reading about that church just the other day. It is a floating house of worship built especially for the Sailor's Mission in Philadelphia. And they are hauling it down there. That's exactly what it is all about."

"Thank goodness," William sighed. "I'm glad I'm not seeing things that aren't there. For a while I was worried about myself."

A moment later George asked, "What banner is that floating from the steeple, Dad? Can you make it out?"

His father watched as the barge moved slowly down the river and out of sight. "No, I can't, George. It may be a sailor's signal flag of some sort but I can't recognize it."

"Is it a Christian flag, Dad?" asked his younger son.

The father answered, "There is no Christian flag that I know of, except the banner someone proposed years ago with Constantine's famous words emblazoned upon it: In Hoc Signo Vinces."

William spoke up immediately, "Which, being translated, means, In this sign, conquer."

George shook his head. "I know you passed Latin, William, but you don't have to throw it in our faces every chance you get. As far as that motto is concerned, it reminds me of the way one boy in our class translated Caesar's 'Veni, Vidi, Vici' once. He said Caesar saw a beautiful Roman maiden one day, and when she invited him to visit her, he said, 'I came, I saw, I concurred.'"

"If that's all the Latin they teach in college," Bishop Doane commented, "someone is going to hear from me. But getting back to that banner on the top of that church, if a Christian flag is ever designed, I hope it will bear Constantine's motto,

42

because it is the most appropriate phrase to adorn such a banner."

"Dad," William exclaimed, after the barge had disappeared from sight, "didn't one of the girls ask you to write a hymn for a flag-raising ceremony next week?"

"Why yes, William, she did," his father answered. "I'd forgotten all about it. Why?"

"Because you could take the story of the banner flying from that church out there and write a hymn about it," his son explained.

"I could indeed," Bishop Doane added. "And I think I will, if you boys will help me."

Doane, the second Episcopal Bishop of New Jersey, was no novice at hymn writing. When only twenty-five years of age, he had published an excellent little volume entitled "Songs by the Way," which included two poetic gems that are regarded to this day as excellent hymns, "Softly now the light of day" and "Thou art the way: to Thee alone," designated "one of the most admirable and useful hymns in the English language" by so great an authority as Dr. John Julian. As founder of St. Mary's Hall, he had pioneered in the field of higher education for girls. Later, in establishing Burlington College, he made provision for training those who desired to take holy orders. The inspiration of seeing a church floating down the river was about all he needed to set his fertile brain to work, since poems and hymns "oozed out in almost everything he said and did." While his boys wrote down the lines, he began to create the hymn for the scheduled flag-raising ceremony at St. Mary's the following week, speaking his phrases dramatically as they came to him:

Fling out the banner! let it float, Skyward and seaward, high
    and wide;
The sun that lights its shining folds, The cross on which the
    Saviour died.

In a few moments, the six stanzas were complete and Bishop Doane had given the Church militant one of its most dynamic hymns.

His ministerial mantle fell upon his younger son, William, who, in 1869, was elected the first Bishop of the Diocese of Albany, New York. The father's talents as a hymn writer were also shared by his second son, because it was William Croswell Doane who, in 1886, wrote the hymn, "Ancient of days, who sittest throned in glory" for the bicentenary of the charter that made Albany the first chartered city in the United States. The second Bishop Doane also wrote a four-volume biography of his distinguished father, following the latter's death at the age of sixty, on April 27, 1859.

The lives of the two men were characterized by a devotion to their calling, expressed so brilliantly in the last stanza of the senior Bishop's hymn:

Fling out the banner! wide and high, Seaward and skyward let
    it shine;
Nor skill, nor might, nor merit ours; We conquer only in that
    sign!

GOD OF OUR FATHERS, WHOSE ALMIGHTY HAND

George William Warren, organist at St. Thomas' Church, New York City, did not know Rev. Daniel Crane Roberts, minister of St. Thomas' Church, Brandon, Vermont. But if ever St. Thomas had ecclesiastical twins (and his name 'Didymus' meant Thomas the Twin, and not Thomas the Doubter), it could well have been the churches named for him in the great metropolis and the tiny village.

The Town Hall at Brandon, Vermont, was to be the scene of a great celebration scheduled for July 4, 1876, when the citizens of the village and surrounding countryside were to gather together to commemorate the one-hundredth anniversary of the signing of the Declaration of Independence. Under the direction of one of the local school teachers, the Dramatic Club planned to re-create the historic scene. Various portions of the Declaration were to be read by some of the boys who were to portray the characters who took part in the actual signing a hundred years earlier. One of the students insisted that he knew the Declaration of Independence by heart. When he explained that he did not need a script for his part in the production, the teacher called his bluff, and said, "If you know the Declaration of Independence by heart, let's have it, word for word, and without a single mistake."

The young boaster took his place in the center of the stage and began reciting these famous lines, "We, the people of the United States, in order to form a more perfect union, establish justice, insure domestic tranquillity, provide for the common defense, promote the general welfare, and secure the blessings of liberty for ourselves and our posterity, do ordain and establish this Constitution—this Constitution—."

He paused amidst roars of laughter. His teacher spoke up.

"We are commemorating the one-hundredth anniversary of the signing of the Declaration of Independence. You are reciting the preamble to the Constitution of the United States, which was not adopted until September 17, 1787, eleven years after the signing of the Declaration of Independence. Now, if you'll just pay attention, we can get on with the rehearsal without further interruption. If anyone else thinks he can recite the Declaration, let him speak now or forever hold his peace."

There being no volunteers, she proceeded without delay. The scheduled skit created a great deal of local interest in the centennial celebration, and caused many adults in the village to go back to their history books and read the actual words themselves, something some of them had never done before.

"The trouble with too many of our people," one townsman remarked, "is that they are always ready to swear by the Declaration of Independence and give their lives to defend the Constitution, when they've never read either one!"

"That's a failing of most Americans," another commented. "It's by no means limited to the folks in Brandon, or Vermont or New England, for that matter."

The Sunday prior to the Fourth of July, 1876, local pastors preached from the text found in Leviticus 25:10, "Proclaim liberty throughout the land, to all the inhabitants thereof," since those were the words on the Liberty Bell. Among those who preached from that verse the Sunday prior to the big event was the minister of St. Thomas' Episcopal Church in Brandon, Rev. Daniel Crane Roberts. The thirty-five-year old rector was a veteran of the Union Army, having fought in the Civil War following his graduation from Kenyon College. At the close of the conflict, he was ordained to the ministry and served two New England parishes before moving to Brandon.

The chairman of the committee arranging the details of the celebration approached Mr. Roberts the middle of June and said, "Mr. Roberts, the members of our general committee have asked me to come to you to see if you would write a new hymn for the centennial. I know this is a rather unusual request, but we want to give the program a religious as well as a patriotic tone, and we thought the introduction of an original hymn by one of our local clergymen would do just that."

"I'm not much of a poet," the young pastor explained, "but I'll be glad to try my hand at it and see what I can do."

"That's very gracious of you, Mr. Roberts. I know you will have something worthy of the occasion," the chairman replied.

"I'll do my best," the minister added. As his interests were primarily in the fields of history and education rather than creative writing and the literary arts, the rector decided at once that the success of the hymn would depend largely upon the tune to which the stanzas were sung. Looking through the Hymnal, he selected the stirring strains of the tune "Russian Hymn," composed by Alexis Lvov in 1833 at the command of the Emperor Nicholas. In the Hymnals, the words "God the All-terrible," or the altered form "God the Omnipotent" were sung to that moving music, and Roberts did not hesitate a moment to select it for his new and as yet unwritten stanzas.

"The music can be arranged for a poem of four lines with ten syllables in each line," he explained to his church organist, "or for a poem of four lines, in which the first and third lines have eleven syllables instead of ten."

With that in mind, he made a half note into two quarter notes, and wrote his poem in 10.10.10.10. meter, four lines with ten syllables in each. Picturing God as the Creator and Upholder of the universe as well as the Guiding Providence behind the formation of the new Republic, he began his hymn with these stirring words:

God of our fathers, whose almighty hand, Leads forth in beauty
   all the starry band
Of shining worlds, in splendor through the skies, Our grateful
   songs before thy throne arise.

"A hymn like this should begin with a blare of trumpets," the committee chairman said, when the young minister read him the new verses.

"I'll settle for the tune known as 'Russian Hymn,' " the pastor replied modestly. And it was to that tune that the new hymn was sung for the first time on July 4, 1876.

When the Episcopal Church appointed a Commission to revise the Hymnal, Roberts sent in his hymn for consideration, but did not sign his name to the paper. When it was accepted, sixty-six-year-old George W. Warren, organist of New York City's St. Thomas' Church, was chosen to compose a fitting tune. With a dramatic flair rarely equalled and never surpassed in the composing of hymn tunes, Warren, in 1892, sixteen years after the words had been written, composed a tune that began with a blare of trumpets. He named his music "National Hymn."

So this hymn, written for the centennial of the Declaration of Independence and used later at the centennial celebration of the adoption of the Constitution, gave its author his one claim to fame. Had he done no more, his life and ministry would have been eminently worthwhile, for his stanzas have won their way into the Hymnals of the Church Universal.

GOD THE OMNIPOTENT

Unusual indeed is the composer who can come up with a masterpiece on order. But one who came through with flying colors was Alexis F. Lvov, a Russian musician who was once lambasted by Wagner, the German, as "a very insignificant person" and praised by Berlioz, the Frenchman, as "a composer of rare talent."

In 1833, when the gifted musical director was thirty-four years of age, he accompanied Emperor (Czar) Nicholas I on his journeys to Prussia and Austria. When the party returned to Moscow, Count Benkendorff informed the son and pupil of the great Feodor Lvov that the sovereign had expressed a regret that the Russian people possessed no national hymn all their own. "He is weary of the English tune that we have been using," said the Count, "and has commissioned you to write a hymn that will be worthy of our people in every way."

As he studied the anthems of other nations, Lvov noted the staid dignity of the British "God save the King," the music of which was then being used by his own people as a stop-gap national. He commented on the originality and fiery movement of the French "Le Marseillaise" as well as the restrained majesty of the Austrian anthem, "Hymn of the Emperor" composed by Haydn in 1797 at the suggestion of the Prime Minister.

"I fully realize the difficulties of the job before me," Lvov said to a fellow musician a few days later. "I am under the necessity of creating a piece of music that will be at the same time robust and stately, as well as stirring and distinctly national in character."

His friend interrupted, "And a composition that will be as fitting in a cathedral in the capital city as in the ranks of the soldiers as they march into battle."

"That I know too well," the future Major-general replied.

"Fortunately there is no promised or threatened penalty if I fail, but if I do, my days here are numbered."

"Remember," his friend added, "your music must appeal to the intelligentsia as well as to the unlettered masses if it is to be a success; to high society as well as to the peasants if it is to become a truly national hymn."

Perplexed by the problem, Lvov puzzled over it and almost concluded that it was beyond his ability. But, while his conscious mind was worrying, his subconscious was going to work. One night, when he returned to his quarters at an unusually late hour, a tune suddenly burst into his brain. On the spur of the moment, he rushed to a piano and hammered out the four lines of the tune he had been commissioned to write. "It is unbelievable," he said when he finished writing down his music. "An hour ago my mind was a perfect blank, and suddenly, seemingly out of nowhere, this tune came crowding in, and lo, here it is, actually down on manuscript paper."

The next day he asked the poet Joukovsky, to suggest some appropriate words for the new tune, but the other man had some difficulty with the lines, especially since the tune was composed for a poem in 11.10.11.9. meter. "The nine syllables of the fourth line seem to destroy the rhythm and balance of the poem," he protested.

But Lvov refused to change a note or a beat. "This is the way the tune came to me and this is the way it is going to stand," he explained to the distraught writer. A few days later, however, he informed Count Benkendorff that the new hymn was all ready. When the Emperor heard the good news, he was elated, and, on November 23, 1833, he came with the Empress and the Grand-Duke to the Court Chapel to hear the new hymn for the first time.

Lvov had wisely assembled a splendidly trained choir to sing the anthem for the Czar and had gathered together two orchestras to back the singers up. After the initial rendition, the monarch asked the composer-conductor to have the combined orchestras play the tune over several times. "It wore well," Lvov commented after that historic performance. "His majesty did not tire of it a single time." The full chorus and orchestra presented the new hymn in its entirety once more, and when the final notes of the last stanza died away, the ruler rose and said, simply, "It is really superb." Turning to Benkendorff, he added, "Count, please inform the Minister of War that I want this hymn adopted by the army as its official hymn." This measure was ratified on December 4, 1833.

Seven days later the first public performance was held at Moscow's Grand Theatre, and met with the enthusiastic approval of the Russian people. On Christman Day it resounded through the halls of the Winter Palace on the occasion of the blessing of the colors.

In appreciation for his work, Nicholas I presented to Alexis Lvov a gold snuff-box adorned with diamonds as a mark of his pleasure. He further ordered that the words "God protect the Czar" be added to the armorial bearings of the composer's family, a distinct and rarely conferred honor.

The famous tune is now found in many hymnals, and to its majestic strains we sing the paraphrase of the Russian anthem which Henry Chorley wrote in 1842, "God the omnipotent, King who ordainest Thunder thy clarion and Lightning thy sword."

Although Lvov composed a great deal of church music before his death in 1870, he is remembered today solely because he was equal to the occasion when his Emperor commanded him to compose a national hymn worthy of the Russian nation. Little did he dream that he was also composing a tune that, with the national hymns of Austria and England, would find a permanent place in the hymnals of Christendom. They should serve to bridge the gulfs and pierce the curtains that separate these various countries each from the other, and bind their people more closely together with the golden cords of Christian love.

HE WHO WOULD VALIANT BE

The King's officer said, "Mr. Bunyan, His Majesty has shown you clemency in the past. You have on several occasions been the recipient of his indulgent grace. Yet you persist in doing that which is unlawful."

"And you have come with a warrant for my arrest, is that it?" the thirty-two-year-old Bunyan asked.

"Yes, Mr. Bunyan," the town constable of Bedford, England replied. He took out an imposing document and began to read. Bunyan looked at his wife and she at him as they tried to catch a few of the words the officer half-read and half-mumbled. "In the year of Our Lord, 1660—yet one John Bunyan of your said town, tinker, hath divers times within one month last past, in contempt of His Majesty's good laws, preached or teached in a conventicle meeting or assembly under color or pretense of exercise of religion in other manner than according to the liturgy or practice of the Church of England."

Bunyan said to his wife, "What was it that Henry VIII said he was going to do? Set up a Church without a Pope? The Pope himself in defense of Romanism could hardly be more cruel than our Monarch in defense of Anglicanism. And there is not too much to choose between them." Then, turning to the visitor, he asked, "Do I plead now or later?"

"You will plead before the Magistrate, Mr. Bunyan, in answer to this warrant for your arrest," the officer stated.

The tinker bade his wife and family "Goodbye" and accompanied the other man to the Bedford jail, which was situated on a narrow bridge that spanned the Ouse River in the center of the town. When Court convened, he pleaded "Guilty," since he had knowingly, consciously and proudly violated a law that he considered not only an affront to man but an insult to God. "There is no such thing as an illegal meeting when Christians of any persuasion gather together to worship God," he said defiantly to the Magistrate. The Judge had no choice in the matter, however, and sentenced him to prison as the law enjoined. He did hold out a possibility of escape, though, by saying to the condemned man, "I will be glad to give you a pardon, Mr. Bunyan, if you will give me your word that you will stop preaching the moment you leave this court room."

Bunyan smiled. "Your Honor," he answered, "if I were out of prison today, I would preach the gospel again tomorrow, by the help of God."

"Take him away," the Magistrate shouted, and Bunyan languished in the local prison for a period of three months. Never a man to let a moment lie idle, he studied the Bible and prepared the sermons he promised to preach the day he was released. Fortunately he had not been fined, else he would have been compelled to spend more months in a debtors' prison. At the time of his marriage, his wife said, "We have neither a spoon nor a dish between us," and the passing of years had done little to increase their supply of wordly goods. While his wife had had no silver or gold to bring him as her "dowry" at the time of their marriage, she had presented him with two books. They had a profound and lasting effect upon her husband's spiritual life, and through him, upon the life of all England.

Revolting with equal fervor against Roman Catholicism on one hand and The Established Church of England on the other, he joined up with those who refused to conform to the King's commands, and were called Non-Conformists, or Dissenters. The Baptists welcomed him with open arms and in their fellowship and service the tinker finally found himself. The members of the small Church at Bedford instructed and inspired him until he felt the call to preach. "I wish to mend people's souls as well as their pots and pans," he said. Now, as a result of the growing popularity of his preaching, he was confined to a dirty cell in a crowded jail. The three months were soon behind him, and immediately upon being set free, his people gathered around him and demanded a sermon. Shortly after preaching, and following the briefest taste of freedom, he found himself back in jail again, under a sentence of twelve years rather than three months. This time he wrote nine books before he was released under a "Declaration of Indulgence" ordered by Charles II. Called to the pastorate of the Bedford Baptist Church, he preached with such power that people were soon referring to him as "Bishop Bunyan." But when Parliament bowed to the will of some powerful reactionaries and revoked the "Declaration," the parson lost his license to preach, was betrayed by some false friends, and arrested and sentenced for the third time in 1675.

It was during this final imprisonment of six months that he began writing his monumental work, "Pilgrim's Progress," first published three years later, in 1678. In his magnificent hymn, "A mighty fortress is our God," written in 1529, the German Reformer, Martin Luther, had sung, "And though this world with devils filled, should threaten to undo us, We will not fear, for God hath willed, His truth to triumph through us." The English world a century and a half later was peopled with the same devils, ghosts and evil spirits as was the German world of Luther. Against them Bunyan waged a constant fight, both as a forceful preacher and as a fluent writer. Following his book's publication and popularity, Bunyan continued the story in companion volumes and enlarged editions of the original. It was for the edition of 1684 that he composed a poem which summed up his beliefs and began, "Who would true valor see, Let him come hither; One here will constant be, Come wind, come weather." He would have been the last man on earth to call himself a hymn writer, although as an allegorist he has had few equals and no peers. It remained for the editors of an English Hymnal two hundred and twenty years later to recast his poem to fit a twentieth-century setting, and their labors resulted in this stirring and dramatic hymn, "He who would valiant be, 'Gainst all disaster, Let him in constancy Follow the Master."

Bunyan's "Pilgrim" had to face discouragement within as well as giants without, but, as long as there loomed before him the vision of the Eternal City, he kept pushing forward. These were the sentiments the poet poured into the only hymn that came from his gifted pen. And those who read his books realized quickly that the writer himself had as thrilling a journey through life as his fictional counterpart, and may have been the Pilgrim of which he wrote so brilliantly. If anyone deserved the welcome, "Enter thou into the joy of thy Lord," it was the tinker who sang in the second stanza of his only hymn, "We know we at the end, Shall life inherit."

HOLY, HOLY, HOLY

When a High Church priest has to work under a Low Church Bishop, a clash is inevitable. However, it usually comes unexpectedly and over the tritest issues. At least that was the case with Britain's famous minister-composer, Rev. John Bacchus Dykes.

This talented and versatile clergyman was awarded the Doctor of Music degree by the University of Durham, England, when he was thirty-eight years of age, in 1861. The very next year he was appointed vicar of St. Oswald's Church, Durham, a post he filled with distinction for fourteen years. The gifted pastor labored long and hard at his new post, and the work of the parish increased as his congregation grew. The hard pressed clergyman carried the load alone as long as he could, and then, in 1873, applied to his Bishop for two curates to assist him. This gave his ecclesiastical superior the chance he had been looking for.

"You are too much of a High Churchman, Dykes," the Bishop said, "and there are some things you do in public worship at St. Oswald's that do not meet with my approval."

Dykes, who was already making a name for himself as a successful composer of hymn tunes, was loathe to enter into an argument over his use of strange liturgical patterns and different materials in the public worship of the Church committed to his care. He merely answered, politely and with restraint, "I am doing what I think is best for my Church and my people. The work of the parish has grown to great proportions and I must have a curate or two to assist me."

The Bishop, though, refused to budge. "Some of the things you are doing smack of Popery," he continued. "I hear that your services are too ritualistic, and some of the parishioners are objecting to these foreign innovations."

"I know we are not in accord, Bishop," Dykes explained,

"but both of us are one in our devotion to our Lord and in our concern for the building up of His Kingdom through the Church. That seems to me to be more important than our differences over the details of our services of public worship."

"That's just it, Dykes," the older man said. "The differences may seem insignificant to you, but they are major differences to me. You may wish to ignore them, but I don't. I think you've gone far enough. In fact, I'd almost be willing to say that I think you have gone too far. Let me give your request a few days' thought. Come back next Wednesday, if you will, and I'll let you know what I have decided to do."

With that, Dykes excused himself and returned to his work at St. Oswald's. The next few days were very busy ones, as the minister was occupied with the usual routine duties that absorb so much of a clergyman's time and energy. The following Wednesday, he showed up at the Bishop's home, prepared to hear him say that he had found a curate or two to aid him in the expanding work of the growing parish. But the Bishop was not in a conciliatory mood. In fact, he was downright pugnacious when he invited his subordinate into the study.

"Dykes," he began, almost before the two could exchange civil greetings, "I've given your request a great deal of study, and I've come to the conclusion that you can have your curates on one condition."

"What is that, Bishop?"

"That you and your assistants sign a paper that I have drawn up."

"Sign a paper? Why? No other priest in the Church of England is required to sign any such document in order to get a curate! What does your paper say?"

The Bishop picked up a sheet of paper from his desk. "It states that you and your assistants agree that the curate shall never wear a colored stole; that you will never have anything to do with incense—"

"Incense?" Dykes asked, half disgusted. "Who ever heard of anyone using incense in our Church?"

"And," continued the Bishop, "you shall never stand with your backs to the congregation except when ordering the Bread for the Sacrament."

"Is that all?" Dykes asked.

"That is all," the Bishop replied.

"It's the most absurd thing I ever heard of," Dykes broke in. "No other priest has to be subjected to such a humiliating experience. I think your action is uncalled for as well as illegal. I refuse to sign any such paper, and will, if necessary, take my plea to the highest Court in the land for settlement." With that, Dykes left the house.

A long and bitter controversy ensued, with the Bishop asserting his authority on the one hand, and Dykes being encouraged by his friends to stand his ground on the other. He pressed the case until it reached the Court of the Queen's Bench. There he pleaded with the justices to issue a writ requiring the Bishop to license the curates without compelling them to sign any such document as the one before them. The Court ruled, on January 19, 1874, that the Bishop had complete authority and sole jurisdiction in such matters.

The shock of this ruling was too much for Dykes to bear. He never recovered from the disappointment, dying two years later in his fifty-third year, on January 22, 1876. His friend said that the blow delivered by the Court killed him. So died the man whose hymn tunes abound in hymnals of all denominations throughout the world.

His famous tune for "Holy, Holy, Holy," penned for Trinity Sunday by Reginald Heber in 1826, was composed in 1861 and named "Nicaea" after the famous Council of Nicaea, 325 A.D. when the doctrine of the Trinity, exalted in Heber's hymn, was fully and finally stated and settled.

That same year he published the tune "Melita" for the hymn known as "The Navy Hymn," "Eternal Father, strong to save," naming his tune after the island of Malta where St. Paul had been shipwrecked. He also composed "Hollingside" for "Jesus, lover of my soul," "Vox Dilecti" for "I heard the voice of Jesus say," as well as the tune "Keble," set to many long meter poems. "Blairgowrie," "St. Andrew of Crete," "St. Agnes," "Dominus Regit Me," "Beatitudo," "Alford," and "Lux Benigna" for "Lead Kindly Light" are among his splendid tunes in common usage throughout the Christian world.

Those who sing them Sunday after Sunday rejoice that "there was a man sent from God whose name was John" who composed the tunes by means of which we might praise and glorify our God as we know Him through Jesus Christ our Lord.

HOW FIRM A FOUNDATION

Some authors and composers try to fool the public by publishing their words under a variety of pen names. The composer of "Whispering Hope," listed as Anne Hawthorne, is none other than the Philadelphia song-writer, Septimus Winner, hiding behind a woman's name. In his own right he was well known in his day as the composer of "Listen to the mocking bird."

As for Fanny Crosby, who penned more than eight-thousand poems and hymns during her ninety-five years, she had more aliases than Public Enemy Number One. Many of her finest poems appeared as the compositions of A.C.; H.D.W.; V.A.; Ella Dale; Jenny V.; Mrs. Jennie Glen; Mrs. Kate Grinley; Grace J.; Henrietta Blair; Rose Atherton and dozens of others, equally anonymous.

Other hymn writers hesitate to sign their names as both author and composer, although a few, like Rev. John H. Hopkins Jr., who gave us the words and music of "We three kings," and Rev. Edwin P. Parker who wrote "Master, no offering costly and sweet," are not embarrassed by that fact.

Henry Ernest Nichol solved the problem to his own satisfaction by using his real name as author, and adopting a pen-name for those hymns for which he also composed the music. He is remembered as the author of "We've a story to tell to the nations," while the composer of the tune to which it is sung is listed as "Colin Sterne." A second glance will reveal that "Sterne" is the poet's name "Ernest" scrambled to suit his taste, while "Colin" is his last name, "Nichol," all mixed up with the "h" left out!

Some poets get credit for other author's successes as was the case with the famous German man of letters, Goethe, who, in many hymnals was credited with having written the hymn, "Purer yet and purer." Research by Professor Alan Pfeffer of the University of Buffalo established the fact that the hymn actually came from the pen of one Anna R. Bennet, and was included in one of her volumes, printed in 1851, and containing, among her original works, some translations from the German writer. Hence the unfortunate mixup which baffled hymnologists for decades.

Again there are poets who are so ashamed of some of their creations that they actually deny them as their own. Rev. Clement Clarke Moore felt that way about his poem, " 'Twas the night before Christmas," saying it was beneath the dignity of a Hebrew Professor in a famous Theological Seminary to admit having written such stuff. But the years proved how wrong he was, and, before he died, he confessed to having penned the only poem by which he is remembered today.

Still others put a strain on historians of the future by affixing only an initial to their writings, to the dismay of those who wish to give them the credit that is their due after the passing of time. Unfortunately we do not even have an initial as a clue to the author of "Come Thou Almighty King" and "We gather together to ask the Lord's blessing." But we do have a letter of the alphabet, and only one, as the signature of the poet who penned the seven thrilling stanzas of the majestic hymn "How firm a foundation." When it was published for the first time in 1787, in "Selection," a collection of hymns prepared by Rev. Dr. John Rippon, minister of a prominent Baptist Church in London at the turn of the nineteenth century, the stanzas appeared under the signature "K." Curious critics dug up dozens of famous names that began with that letter, from Kirkham to Keith, and from Kingsbury to Keene. But, while a majority of them agreed that "Keene" could have been Robert Keene, the director of music in Dr. Rippon's Church at the time, his authorship has never been fully established beyond a reasonable doubt, and the creator of one of the noblest hymns of the Church continues to be listed as "Anonymous."

As if that were not enough, the name of the composer of the tune to which these stanzas are sung, "Adeste Fidelis," is wrapped in the same cloak of anonymity. For sometime after it was first published in John F. Wade's volume, "Cantus Diversi," in England in 1751, it was called "Portuguese Hymn," leaving some with the erroneous impression that it originated in

Portugal. Later it was established that the music had been discovered and used in the Chapel of the Portuguese Embassy in London, and had no connection with the country from which the ambassador had come.

Even the Christmas hymn, "O come, all ye faithful," which is wedded to the same excellent tune in the hearts of Christians all over the world, was authored by an unknown poet. Supposedly it came from the pen of an eighteenth century French or German writer, but its translation into English by Canon Frederick Oakeley in 1841 assured it a permanent place in Christian hymnody.

The most important fact about the two hymns and the tune to which they are sung is not that their creators are unknown, but that they themselves knew Him of whom they wrote and sang. It was for that reason that "How firm a foundation" was the favorite hymn of President Theodore Roosevelt, as well as President Andrew Jackson, who requested that it be sung during his last and fatal illness. For that reason, too, it was the special favorite of that southern gentleman without peer, Robert E. Lee, who asked that it be sung at his funeral "as an expression of his full trust in the ways of the Heavenly Father."

When earth's final secrets are revealed and her deepest mysteries unravelled, many will rejoice to know the names of the unknown authors and composers whose hymns made many weak Christians become towers of strength, and sustained others by encouraging them to lean heavily upon a God who would never forsake them, but would be with them to the very end.

I AM SO GLAD THAT JESUS LOVES ME

Sometimes it is the cruel fate of good poets and musicians to have their greatness obscured by some bit of doggerel that makes their names appear ridiculous to those who know them not. A prominent columnist for a leading Chicago newspaper recently printed a poem entitled "The Ashtabula Disaster" by one Julia Moore, "The sweet singer of Michigan." A sorrier piece of poetry would be difficult to find and a more tragic misunderstanding of history on the part of the columnist hard to come by.

The four stanzas and chorus of Julia's ditty recount, in unbalanced meter and crude phraseology, the terrible railroad accident at Ashtabula, Ohio, when the well known song leader and composer, Philip P. Bliss, and his wife lost their lives. Commenting on this trashy bit of verse, the writer adds an explanatory poem of his own which begins with these lines: "Ashamed am I to tell you this: I never heard of P. P. Bliss—Nor even P. P. Bliss's wife—Never once in all my life." And in that way he dismisses from history one of the most unusual, talented and prolific gospel song writers the nation has produced. As for the author of the doggerel, her reputation for gory lyrics was so well-known that a critic commented on her first published volume in these caustic words, "I counted twenty-one dead and nine wounded."

But Bliss deserves a better fate, because the songs and hymns he wrote will live as long as the Church lives. Next to Fanny Crosby, he authored more successful gospel songs than any other person in American Church history. While unchurched newscolumnists pass him off with a shrug of the shoulder, millions of Christians rise up and call him blessed everytime they open a hymnal or a songbook.

In June, 1870, Mr. and Mrs. Bliss were guests in the home of Major D. W. Whittle, at 43 South May Street, Chicago. The musician had been employed for several years by Dr. George F. Root, during which time he had devoted himself to conducting singing schools and musical institutes and composing Sunday School songs for publication. One evening during their visit at the Whittle's, the conversation turned to the subject of children's hymns and songs. Mr. Bliss spoke enthusiastically of a tune which his employer had composed several years earlier. "Dr. Root composed his beautiful tune for W. O. Cushing's words back in 1856," he said. "Cushing had written what he called 'The Jewel Song' which began, 'When he cometh, when he cometh, to make up his jewels.' And Root decided that it would make an excellent children's hymn. Personally I think he did an unusually fine job of it, don't you, Major Whittle?" His host agreed and did the others who were sitting about the living room.

Bliss continued, "Cushing also wrote 'Down in the valley with My Saviour I would go' and 'Ring the bells of heaven,' but I think 'Jewels' is by far the finest thing he has produced."

Mrs. Bliss asked, "What about 'Jesus loves me, this I know?' Isn't that still the children's favorite?"

"Beyond a doubt," her husband replied. "That was published three years after 'Jewels.' Anna Warner wrote the words and included them in her novel 'Say and Seal' which was published in 1859. But with those two notable exceptions the children are practically ignored by modern hymn writers."

Later, with those words burning in his heart, the Blisses excused themselves, went to their room and prepared to retire. Bliss lay on his bed deep in thought far into the night, and gradually found himself picking out phrases and matching the lines with a simple melody that seemed to come simultaneously with the words. Very early in the morning, he awoke his wife and sang a stanza and chorus of the new song to her. She nodded a drowsy approval, turned over and went back to sleep.

When Mrs. Bliss came down to breakfast the following morning she said to her host, "Last evening Mr. Bliss had a tune given to him that I think is going to live and be one of the most used that he has written. I have been singing it all the morning to myself and cannot get it out of my mind." When her host urged her to share the new song with him, she sang the first stanza and chorus of her husband's latest song. When the composer joined them at the table a short while later, his host greeted him and commented enthusiastically upon the new song, "I am so glad that Jesus loves me."

"What gave you the idea, Mr. Bliss?" Major Whittle asked. The musician replied, "The consciousness that the peace and comfort of the Christian were not founded upon his loving Christ but upon Christ's love for him. To occupy the mind with Christ's love would produce love and consecration in keeping with Romans 5:5, 'The love of God is shed abroad in our hearts by the Holy Ghost which is given to us.'"

While it is more important for an adult to know that God believes in him whether he believes in God or not, it is likewise essential for us always to remember that God in Christ Jesus loves us whether we love him or not. It was in that spirit and with that desire that Bliss wrote his children's hymn which now ranks with 'Jewels' and 'Jesus loves me' as one of the three best children's hymns in Christendom.

I HEARD THE VOICE OF JESUS SAY

Dwight L. Moody walked to the front of the platform and faced the thousands of people who filled Edinburgh's Free Assembly Hall to capacity that evening in 1874. "With us on the platform today," he said, "is a man who needs no introduction to a Scottish congregation. The distinguished man of God is known far and wide as a fearless preacher, an accomplished writer and a talented poet and hymn writer. Since 1866 he has been the pastor of the Chalmers' Memorial Free Church here in Edinburgh. We will now hear from Dr. Horatius Bonar."

The sixty-six-year-old minister spoke only a few minutes, but, in the words of those present, "he spoke with great power, thrilling the immense audience with his eloquence." Since Mr. Moody had announced that "The Good Shepherd" would be his theme for the evening, Dr. Bonar dwelt briefly on that majestic theme from the New Testament. The stage was now set for one of the most unusual and dramatic events in the history of Christian hymnody.

Moody turned to his song leader, Ira D. Sankey, and asked, "Have you a solo appropriate for this subject?"

It was then that Sankey, under the inspiration of The Holy Spirit, took out a poem he had clipped from a Glasgow newspaper the day before, went to the organ and began singing spontaneously, composing the music as he went along, Elizabeth Clephane's hymn "The Ninety and Nine." Had Dr. Bonar done nothing else than inspire Sankey to sing that song, his life and ministry would have been outstanding. Because the atmosphere he created made it possible for the singer to give the wings of music to the poet's lines, giving the world a song that won more people to Christ than all the other labors of the preacher and singer combined. But Bonar was more than an inspirer of hymns and gospel songs. Moody had told Sankey, "Dr. Bonar is the greatest hymn writer in Scotland today. As one of the leaders in the Free Church movement, he is held in high respect by the Scottish people. He told me that it was originally his desire to remain in Kelso the rest of his life, serving the Church there. But, after a twenty-nine year pastorate, serving the North Parish under the Established Church, and later the Free Church there, following the Disruption in May, 1843, he felt called to accept the pastorate at Edinburgh. The city is fortunate to have a man of his calibre and consecration in one of her most influential pulpits."

When Sankey inquired as to the history of the Disruption, Moody explained, "The Established Church of Scotland is the Presbyterian Church. In the late 1830s a controversy arose over the right of a Presbytery to compel a congregation to take a pastor to whom the majority of the members were opposed. Many ministers felt that the Presbytery had no such authority, and sought to adopt a rule to that effect. The case was carried to the law-making body of the Church, the General Assembly, and eventually to the Parliament in London, which always has the final word. As a result of being rebuffed, 474 of these ministers, under the leadership of Rev. Dr. Thomas Chalmers, withdrew from the Established Church and organized The Free Church of Scotland, in May, 1843. This was a daring move, because the Established Church is supported by the government and bills are paid from taxes levied on the people. Bonar was one of the supporters of this move, since he and Chalmers, his former teacher, were close friends."

Although Bonar was only thirty-five at the time of the Disruption, he was already hailed as one of the most capable ministers and scholars in the Church. As for his hymns, he said, "They come to me at such odd times and sometimes I am compelled to jot them down on odd pieces of paper. About the only time I have left to concentrate on writing hymns is the time I spend riding on railroad trains to and from preaching and speaking appointments." Consequently many of his six-hundred hymns were penned aboard a train by a travelling preacher who did not have the time to polish them once they were written down.

"Go labor on, spend and be spent," usually designated his first accepted hymn now in general use, was written the same year he withdrew from the Established Church, during his ministry in Kelso. That it is descriptive of his own life is seen in these varied comments about him by many different people, which were actually compliments in disguise, "He is always preaching," "He is always visiting," "He is always writing" and "He is always praying."

While the above hymn was written for the adults in his congregation, his finest, "I heard the voice of Jesus say," was inspired by his love of the "little lambs" of the flock, and came from his pen several years prior to its first publication in the poet's "Hymns Original and Selected," 1846. "I want the children in my Sunday School to know Jesus as the supreme giver of rest, as the water of life and as the light of the world, because all people are tired, thirsty and wanderers in the dark. I know no better way to teach them these truths than by incorporating them in a hymn which the children can understand and can learn to sing and to love," he said as he introduced this gem to his people for the first time.

Even his wife, Jane Lundie Bonar, whom he married in 1843, found his poetic fire contagious, and wrote a hymn of her own which appeared in the second edition of "Songs for the wilderness," 1846. As altered, it is now called "Fade, fade each earthly joy, Jesus is mine," and is still sung in many parts of Christendom. She was not the only poet on her side of the family, however, because her sister, Mary, who married Rev. William Duncan, had written "Jesus, tender shepherd, hear me," in 1839, prior to her untimely death the very next year.

Bonar's communion hymn came about as a result of a custom of many years standing whereby he and his minister brother, John James Bonar, of St. Andrew's Free Church, Greenock, celebrated Communion together once a year. Young Bonar wrote, "Here, O my Lord, I see thee face to face," at his brother's request for their service scheduled for the first Sunday in October, 1855, and it was printed in the bulletin prepared for that occasion. Renowned as an editor and author in addition to his fame as a preacher and hymn writer, Bonar was honored by his Church when elected to fill its highest office, that of Moderator of the General Assembly, in 1883, six years before his death in July, 1889.

Of his one hundred hymns now in common usage, these three have that enduring quality which endears them to Christians and insures their constant and continued use by believers of all ages for many years to come. Between the hymns he inspired and those he wrote, his biographer could say of him, with justifiable pride, "He wrought a good work for Jesus Christ."

I LOVE TO STEAL AWHILE AWAY

Kittenish kids may be cute, but if they grow up to become catty women, that's a different story. Because there is nothing cute or cultured about the way such women can tear into other women, and claw them and their families and reputations to bits without batting an eye.

One such wealthy and aristocratic woman attended a tea at the home of Dr. Hyde in Ellington, Connecticut, one afternoon in August, 1818. As she mingled with the guests, she caught a glimpse of Mrs. Phoebe Hinsdale Brown, the wife of a house-painter, Timothy Brown, whose humble back yard adjoined the lower garden of her own spacious estate. Walking over to her in a very haughty manner, she asked, in a voice loud enough to be heard by everyone present, "Why, how do you do, Mrs. Brown? It's so nice to see you."

"Thank you," the other woman replied, softly and with evident respect.

"I hope you and your family are well," she continued, raising her voice so all could get the benefit of the conversation without having to strain themselves.

"Very well, thank you," Mrs. Brown replied.

"Mrs. Brown," her neighbour continued, in a very condescending tone, "tell me, why do you walk down through your yard every evening and come up so close to our house and then turn and go back without speaking to any of us?"

Mrs. Brown could feel the eyes of the other guests staring at her. "I've been in the habit of walking down there every evening for several months, because it is so cool and quiet," she explained.

"Well," her neighbour continued, "we couldn't imagine who would be walking down there in the twilight like that, night after night. So I sent my little girl down to the lower garden to see who it was. She came back and said that it was you, and that you came down to the fence, and then turned quickly when you saw her there and walked back to your own house."

"Oh," Mrs. Brown said, almost on the verge of tears. "I didn't know anyone saw me, or heard me. I'm sorry if my twilight rambles have been a matter of concern to you or to any other neighbours." Turning to her host, Mrs. Brown said, "Dr. Hyde, I wonder if you would excuse me? This has been a very pleasant and a very delightful afternoon. Thank you so much for inviting me to be present."

Dr. Hyde walked with her to the door. "We are glad you could come, Mrs. Brown. Please come again soon, and bring your precious children next time."

"Thank you, Dr. Hyde. I will."

As she left the house, Mrs. Jackson, one of her closest friends, caught up with her. "I'll walk home with you, Phoebe," she said, as she took her arm. "I heard every word that old hen had to say. If that is culture and aristocracy, I don't want any part of it."

But the well-to-do neighbour didn't let the matter drop when Mrs. Brown left. To her it was too good a morsel not to chew on over and over again, cud-like. As some of the others gathered around, she said, "I never could understand that Mrs. Brown. I can't imagine why she walks down there every evening like she does. Why, the way some people talk—."

"You mean, you think she may be having an affair with somebody? Does she meet him down there after dark?" another woman asked.

"You can never tell," the ring-leader replied, adding fuel to the fire. "I've seen just about enough. As far as I'm concerned, what people are saying is true. The very idea of her flaunting her infidelity in our faces like that. Something ought to be done about women like her," she said, as they walked back into the living room, preening themselves like peacocks, so proud of their unruffled feathers, their sterling characters and their aristocratic dignity.

Mrs. Brown said to Mrs. Jackson, as she walked up on the porch of her own humble home, "Something ought to be done about women like her. They have no idea how much damage they do, how much pain and heartache they cause by their idle gossip, and how many people they hurt by jumping to hasty and unproven conclusions. It grieves me to think that she is so utterly incapable of appreciating the object of my visits to the garden in the cool of the evening to commune with God and pray. To think she has imputed an immoral motive to my twilight rambles."

Mrs. Jackson put a loving arm about her. "Those of us who know you and Timothy and the children," she said, "don't put any stock in what other people say. So don't shed any tears over it, Phoebe. It isn't worth it. I know how it is with Timothy working one week and being laid off the next, and so many mouths to feed and bodies to clothe, and how you've been taking care of your invalid sister all these months when you haven't a bed or a mouthful of food to spare. If other people want to think their ugly and dirty thoughts, let them. It's between them and their God. After all, they are only hurting themselves."

Later that night, when the rest of the family were fast asleep, thirty-five-year-old Phoebe Hinsdale Brown sat at the kitchen table. "I know what I'll do," she said, half-aloud. "I'll write an apology and explain to her just what I've been doing. She has misunderstood me so. Maybe when she reads my letter she will be a bit more understanding and sympathetic. If she has a tender heart, possibly I can touch it with a poem, and then she won't think so harshly of me any more."

Picking up a piece of paper and a pen, she wrote at the top of the page, "An Apology for my Twilight Rambles, Addressed to a Lady, Ellington, August 1818." Under that caption she wrote a poem containing nine simple four-line stanzas. The first two stanzas were:

Yes, when the toilsome day is gone, And night, with banners
    gray,
Steals silently the glade along, In twilight's soft array,
I love to steal awhile away, From little ones and care,
And spend the hours of setting day, In gratitude and prayer.

Six years later, Dr. Nettleton selected this poem for inclusion in the 1824 edition of his book "Village Hymns." As altered by him, the first stanza was eliminated, and the second revised to read:

I love to steal awhile away, From every cumbering care,
And spend the hours of closing day, In humble, grateful prayer.

The second, fifth, seventh and ninth stanzas of her original poem are now included in many hymnals, and prized as one of the finest devotional poems in Christian literature.

Mrs. Brown lived to see one of her sons, Dr. S. R. Brown, go out as the first American missionary to Japan, before she passed away in Henry, Illinois, in 1861, her seventy-eighth year. She died in the spirit of the last stanza of her famous "Apology," which reads:

Thus, when life's toilsome day is o'er, May its departing ray
Be calm as this impressive hour, And lead to endless day.

I LOVE TO TELL THE STORY

The audience did not know what to expect when Major-General Russell stood up to speak. Everyone attending the International Y.M.C.A. convention in Montreal, Canada, the summer of 1867, knew him by reputation, because he was in command of British troops who were charged with putting down insurrections and breaking up riots in Ireland. The popular excitement over the Irish "home rule" issue made whatever the General planned to say of unusual public interest. Everyone listened intently as he began speaking in a quiet, subdued tone of voice.

"There's nothing military about him," one young man said to a companion. "He can't even bark an order."

"Hush," his friend replied. "He's getting ready to speak."

"My friends," Russell began, "I am not here to make an address or a speech, nor am I present at this convention to explain or defend a particular point of view with regard to what some may consider a very pressing national issue. This afternoon, I merely want to read to you a very beautiful poem which I came across recently, which should be the dominant theme undergirding everything we do here."

With that, he took a piece of paper from his pocket, and began to read, with deep emotion:

> Tell me the old, old story, Of unseen things above,
> Of Jesus and His glory, Of Jesus and His love.

As he finished reading the fourth stanza, tears were streaming down his cheeks. Many of those present were also deeply moved by the simplicity and sincerity of the words, among them being Dr. William H. Doane, the well-known composer from the United States.

He went to General Russell's room later that evening and requested a copy of the stanzas. At the same time he asked the Britisher about the author.

"Her name," General Russell explained, "is really Arabella Catherine Hankey, but we know her familiarly as Kate Hankey; and she is the daughter of a prominent English banker."

"What does she do? Where did she get the inspiration for her poem?" Doane asked.

"She is now thirty-three years of age, I believe," the other man continued, "and as far as I know, she devotes most of her time and attention to organizing and conducting Bible classes among high class as well as low class women and girls in England. Last year she was quite ill, but refused to remain idle, even though she had to spend a great deal of time in bed. During that time she worked on a long poem of some fifty stanzas, dealing with the Life of Our Lord. She published the first part under the title, 'The Story Wanted,' in 1866, last year, in January. The poem I read is taken from that portion of her work. The second section, 'The Story Told,' came from the publishers last November, and the third part 'The Story Welcomed' was printed a few months ago. You see, her lines, 'For I am weak and weary' were autobiographical, because that was her true physical condition when she wrote the words."

Dr. Doane took the stanzas with him when he returned to the States. Some months later, while riding on a stage-coach through the White Mountains, he received the inspiration for his music, the Chorus being his own contribution. The evening of that same day, he wrote his tune down and sang it for friends in the living room of the Crawford House.

In the second part of Miss Hankey's work, song-writer William G. Fischer (1835-1912) found another poem which he felt would make a splendid gospel song. The words began:

I love to tell the story, Of unseen things above;
Of Jesus and His glory; Of Jesus and His Love.

Although it was very much like "Tell me the old, old story," containing the same imagery and thought, Fischer made a copy of the stanzas in order to set them to music. He carried the words with him for quite a while, but a satisfactory tune seemed to elude him. Finally, in 1869, two years after Doane had set the other part to music, he picked out what he thought would be a good melody, but the song still seemed incomplete. One night, during a period of restlessness, the music of the Chorus came to him. Immediately he realized that that was just what the song needed. He hastened to complete the manuscript and send it off to the publishers. To his surprise, it became the most popular tune he ever composed.

His daughter, Blanche W. Fischer, telling about her father's early years, took especial delight in recalling that when he was a lad only eight years old he was asked to lead the singing in his local Sunday School, since he could carry a tune better than anyone else attending regularly. The boy agreed to help, although he had to stand on a chair to be seen and heard by the assembled scholars. She told of the thrills she shared with him after her mother's death, when she travelled with him as he went all over the country. He was invariably recognized, called to the platform and introduced as "the composer of 'I love to tell the story.'"

Of his more than two hundred or more gospel songs, this one is by far the best, although many hymnals include his "Whiter than snow," and "The rock that is higher than I" as well as "I am coming to the cross."

Although Miss Hankey and composers Fischer and Doane died within three years of each other, the songs they wrote between them will never die, because their simplicity, directness and emotional appeal will continue to make them dear to the hearts of Christian people until "the old, old story of Jesus and His love" is told as far as the curse of sin is found.

I WOULD BE TRUE

"A creed is what you believe, or what you don't believe," the young English professor, Howard Arnold Walter, explained to his class. "And everyone has a creed, whether he realizes it or not. Your creed is what you live by," the twenty-three-year-old Princeton graduate continued, as he spoke to his class at Waseda University, Tokyo, Japan, that spring afternoon in 1906. "And a creed does not have to be a dead and lifeless thing either. Of necessity it must be brief, but that doesn't mean it cannot contain a kernel of truth."

The students listened attentively as the youthful American teacher explained how the statement of Christian faith known as "The Apostles' Creed" came into existence, and analyzed it for them phrase by phrase. "Look at it this way," he said. "When I write a letter to my mother back in the United States, I usually close by writing 'love and kisses' or else I put a few X marks at the bottom of the page, because that stands for 'love and kisses.' Now those X marks do not tell her of all the love I hold for her, but they are little symbols of a lot of love, and she knows what they mean and is made happy. In somewhat the same way, the phrases of this Creed do not exhaust Christian truth; they merely hint at it. They are symbols of the greater truths that cannot be limited to words or adequately expressed in phrases or even paragraphs. They are like the X marks at the bottom of my letter—symbols of a reality that cannot be reduced to words, that is almost inexpressibly great and can only be hinted at by Christian people."

The talented young "foreigner" was thrilled when the invitation to teach in Japan came to him following his graduation from Hartford Theological Seminary in Connecticut, and was enjoying his experiences in The Land Of The Rising Sun to the full. The evening after his discussion of creeds, he began to think seriously of trying to reduce his basic, fundamental Christian convictions to a few brief, concise statements. "I want to try my hand at writing my own creed," he explained to a fellow-teacher the next afternoon. "Some people say that the Bible is their creed, but that statement takes in so much territory that it really doesn't mean anything at all. Others say that they have no creed, but that only proves that they are trying to build their lives on negatives rather than positives. As for me, I want to know what I am here for, and why, and what God expects of me and how I can fulfil His will for my life."

The next few days were busy ones, occupied with teaching and sight-seeing and trying to interpret the United States to his Japanese hosts in many different and varied gatherings. But Walter began to jot down a few words in his notebook every now and then, listing them under the caption "My Creed." The following Sunday he glanced at the page and discovered that he had written down these words, among others: True, Pure, Strong, Brave, Friendly, Liberal, Humble, Helpful. Suddenly the whole thing crystallized in his mind. He sat down at his desk and began to write out his creed in the form of a poem. His first lines read as follows:

I would be true, for there are those who trust me;
I would be pure, for there are those who care.

When he laid his pen down on the desk, he had written two four-line stanzas, closing with these words:

I would be humble, for I know my weakness,
I would look up, and laugh, and love, and lift.

"I want to know what I believe," he said later, when he read the stanzas to a close friend, "but I also want to know why and for what purpose, for what end, for what goal. That's why I wrote my poem as I did."

Walter mailed a copy of his poem to his mother, Mrs. Martha A. Walter, back in the States, in a letter dated July 1, 1906. She was so moved by them that, unbeknown to her son, she sent a copy to the editor of Harper's "Bazaar." "I feel that the lines my son wrote merit wider circulation," she stated in the letter that accompanied the poem. The editors agreed and published the poem early in 1907.

The young minister returned home the following year to begin his work as a Congregational preacher. During the summer of 1909 he supplied the pulpit of the Nostrand-DeKalb Methodist Church in Brooklyn, New York. Among the members of the congregation was a sixty-six-year-old former florist, Joseph Yates Peek, currently serving as a lay preacher, conducting services in Churches throughout the country. He was deeply impressed by Walter's sincerity of purpose and the two men became fast friends, despite the disparity of their ages. When the young minister gave his friend a copy of "My Creed," Peek felt that it was too good not to be sung. While he did not boast of a formal musical education, he was a fairly good amateur violinist and pianist. During the next few days he set himself to the task of composing a suitable tune for his friend's poem. When he thought he had it, he went to an organist friend, Dr. Tuller, and asked him to write down the music while he whistled what he had in mind. Between the two of them, they managed to get the music on paper and harmonized in four parts. Just as Peek had predicted all along, the moment the words were set to music, their message began to spread far and wide.

In 1913, John R. Mott asked Walter to join the staff of the Y.M.C.A. and undertake work among students in India and Ceylon. His physician tried to dissuade him from accepting, due to a serious heart condition from which he had suffered for several years. But he accepted the challenge, and went to India, setting up headquarters in Lahore. However, before he could plunge into the work to which he had dedicated himself, God called him home quite suddenly, on November 1, 1918, during his thirty-fifth year.

Young people the world over mourned his passing, but rejoiced that he had had the desire to reduce his creed to poetic form, so that they could take his words and make them their own, and grow up to take the place of him whom God had summoned to "nobler work above."

IN THE GARDEN

Some poets and composers have made fortunes for everyone but themselves, while others have been smart enough to "clean up" while the getting was good. On the other hand, some musicians don't know whether to sell a song outright and pocket the cash or take a chance on royalties from future sales.

John Philip Sousa, the famous bandmaster, faced that situation twice, and must have resolved the conflict with a flip of a coin, because he sold his "Washington Post March" outright for $35. Later he took a chance on publishing his equally well-known march, "Stars And Stripes Forever" on a royalty basis and pocketed more than $300,000.

A few years ago an American band leader sued two popular composers for $600,000, alleging plagiarism in connection with their popular song success, "Buttons And Bows." A Los Angeles Superior Court Jury ruled that the basic melody of the song was in the public domain, thus depriving the band leader of a larger fortune than Bach, Beethoven and Brahms had amassed in their entire lifetimes.

That is a far cry from the troubles that beset a British songwriter, James Alexander Balfour Campbell Tyrie, in September of 1953. While his name may not be as familiar to American audiences as it is to British theater-goers, people on both sides of the Atlantic sing his two famous songs with equal gusto, because the man with the five names composed "Show me the way to go home" and the perennial favorite "Let me call you sweetheart." That fateful September morning he was sentenced to a year in a hospital and put on three years probation for leaving a hotel without paying an $8 bill that he owed. The magistrate actually ordered him to repay the hotel the money he had "swindled" from them. What happened to the cash that must have poured in from his song successes is anybody's guess!

There is additional irony in the fact that the first complete version of the national anthem, "The Star Spangled Banner," by Francis Scott Key, sold for $26,428.00 in Baltimore recently, when it was purchased and turned over to the Maryland Historical Society as the centerpiece for a permanent memorial to the lawyer-poet. At that, it brought more than the original manuscript of Reginald Heber's famous missionary hymn, "From Greenland's Icy Mountains," which sold for a mere $210.00, a sum reputed to be much larger than the special missionary offering it was written to inspire in May of 1819.

As for C. Austin Miles, he didn't know a good thing when he wrote it. After putting the finishing touches on his new gospel song back in 1912, he offered it to the Hall-Mack Publishing Company. The publishers took one look at the song, entitled "In The Garden," decided to take a big gamble, and gave the author-composer the magnificent sum of $4 for it, which amounted to a dollar each for the three stanzas with an extra dollar thrown in for the chorus. By the time of the author's death at the age of seventy-eight, the song had been printed more than three million times, and recordings had topped the millon mark. If he had only been as smart as Sousa and offered it for publication on a royalty basis, he would either have had it thrown back in his face or else would have made a fortune! It's almost a case of "heads I win, tails you lose."

Of his more than thirty-thousand hymn and song tunes, "In The Garden" is far and away the most popular. And he didn't die a pauper, because he served as music editor of the Rodeheaver Hall-Mack Company for more than forty-three years.

Such was not the case with the Rev. Thomas O. Chisholm, of Vineland, New Jersey, author of the gospel song, "Great is thy faithfulness." The faithfulness of God was, to him, almost in direct contrast to the faithlessness of man! He was so hard pressed financially that he was even dropped from The Gideons for "non-payment of dues." The poet and his wife were indeed in dire straits one night in 1941. In their prayers before retiring they told God of their condition and asked Him to remember them. Unknown to the two, a New York City businessman had had them on his heart, although he knew the minister only through his hymns and poems. He sent them a check through an attorney whom he had asked to find the aged couple and forward the money to them. "It was an example of God's faithfulness," the pastor said upon receiving the unexpected, badly needed funds. In May of 1949 he wrote "I am nearly eighty-three years of age, but strength from above has been supplied together with the fulfillment of the promise 'My God shall supply all your need.' Not only the supply of the need but the timing of help has signalized the tokens of His providential care."

Some would say that Rev. Mr. Chisholm was wealthier with a faith like that than those more fortunate authors and composers who have made fortunes only to waste them in riotous living and end out their days devoid of both money and the sustaining faith of a true believer.

IN THE HOUR OF TRIAL

"The prisoner will rise," the bailiff shouted. Twenty-three-year-old James Montgomery looked about the courtroom for the sympathetic face of a friend, but the room was almost empty except for a few hangers-on who had nothing else to do that morning in the fall of 1794. He rose slowly, turned to face the judge who was presiding over the court in Sheffield, England, and remained standing to hear the sentence pronounced.

"Mr. Montgomery," the judge began, "the charge against you is a serious one. England and France are at peace, in spite of the fact that France is now in the midst of a rather violent revolution."

The young newspaper editor started to speak, but the judge held up his hand and silenced him with a gesture.

"We cannot afford to permit newspapermen like yourself to unduly excite the British people, or, by means of your columns, to incite them to take sides in French internal affairs."

"But, your honor," Montgomery objected, "you are denying the freedom of the press."

"That may be your personal opinion, Mr. Montgomery, but this court holds a different view. And, for printing in the columns of your newspaper, 'The Sheffield Iris,' a poem celebrating the fall of the Bastille in Paris at the hands of an unruly mob, this court sentences you to serve three months in the local jail, and fines you the sum of twenty pounds ($100)."

"Your honor," the young writer protested, "Britain is already trying to raise an army for the inevitable war with France once the revolution is over. She has already taken sides. The Government may be neutral, but the people are not. They are on the side of the French people who are justified in taking up arms against their decadent and corrupt rulers."

"Enough!" shouted the judge. "Take the prisoner away!"

Languishing in the dirty confines of the Sheffield prison,

Montgomery had plenty of time to recall the chain of circumstances that had brought him so low, when he had aimed so high! He remembered the day he had gone to London in high hopes of finding a publisher for his poems, and his disappointment when no one had showed any interest in his literary efforts. Then, in 1792, he had accepted an invitation from Mr. Gales, the editor of 'The Sheffield Register,' to become his assistant, and eagerly plunged into the newspaper business with all of his youthful enthusiasm. But Mr. Gales had had cold feet, and had fled the country early in 1794, fearing the fate that his assistant now faced. Montgomery had then bought the paper, changed its name, and set out to recoup his fortune and his reputation. But hardly six months had passed, and now he was in prison. As for the fine, unless some friends came to his rescue, he would have to serve additional time in a debtor's prison for that unpaid obligation. But his friends rallied to his support, raised the $100, and, three months later, Montgomery was a free man again, little the worse for his incarceration.

Some people in Sheffield said, "I hope this taught the editor a lesson." But unfortunately it had not. Two years later, in 1796, he was in the same courtroom again. The judge regarded him sternly, and said, "Mr. Montgomery, the court thought you had learned your lesson, but apparently you newspapermen are a hard lot. You have carried a detailed account of a workingman's riot in a Sheffield mill in your paper, which this court considers inimical to the public interest. And, to impress upon you the seriousness of the charge, this court sentences you to serve six months in the local jail and imposes upon you a fine of thirty pounds ($150)."

Like John Bunyan who wrote "Pilgrim's Progress" in Bedford jail over a century earlier, Montgomery spent this time writing, producing a successful volume entitled "Prison Amusements." Coming out six months later something of a celebrity, he discovered that the circulation of his paper had grown by leaps and bounds, and he was almost tempted to write a letter to the local judge, thanking him for being afforded the privilege of the second prison experience!

Thereafter, he devoted his talents to writing, lecturing and championing many varied causes, from foreign missions to the abolition of the slave trade, and from humanizing the lot of the chimney-sweep to encouraging the widespread use of the Bible. All of these activities resulted in his being recognized as the first citizen of Sheffield.

Like Joseph Addison, who printed many of his original hymns in the columns of his newspaper, "The Spectator," Montgomery carried one of his Christmas hymns, "Angels from the realms of glory," in the columns of "The Sheffield Iris" in the issue of December 24, 1816. From his fluent pen came the beautiful hymn, "Prayer is the soul's sincere desire," written in 1818 at the request of the Rev. Mr. Bickersteth, and the stirring stanzas of "Hail to the Lord's anointed," composed shortly before Christmas, 1821.

It was during his sixty-third year, on October 13, 1834 to be exact, that he was inspired to write one of his noblest hymns. Reading through the Gospels, he came again upon the story of Peter's denial and thought of his own experiences years earlier when he had been tempted to forgo the humiliation of imprisonment for standing up for his convictions. He read again the words of Jesus to the impulsive fisherman, "I have prayed for you that your faith fail not," and followed the story to its bitter climax of denial and its conclusion when Jesus, with a look, recalled Peter to service in His Kingdom. Linking his own experiences with that of the familiar New Testament story, he began to write:

In the hour of trial, Jesus, plead for me; Lest by base denial, I
    depart from Thee;
When Thou seest me waver, With a look recall; Nor for fear or
    favor, Suffer me to fall.

He wrote many books and numerous hymns, among them, "God is my strong salvation," "Go to dark Gethsemane," "The Lord is my shepherd, no want shall I know," "Sow in the morn thy seed," and "Jerusalem, my happy home." Next to Wesley and Watts, more of his hymns are in general use than those of any other hymn writer.

The son of Moravian missionary parents, both of whom died on foreign soil, Montgomery lived a long and useful life, dying in his eighty-third year, April 30, 1854, at his home in Sheffield, after a beautiful and serene old age. He passed away in the spirit of one of his own stanzas:

Prayer is the Christian's vital breath, The Christian's native air, His watchword at the gates of death; He enters heaven with prayer.

Though they imprisoned his body, his spirit and mind were forever free. Such has always been the lot of the true Christian in all conditions and circumstances of life.

IN THE SECRET OF HIS PRESENCE

"I won't go; you understand? I don't want to go back to India and teach my own people," Ellen Lakshmi Goreh said to her English foster parents. "I'm happy here in England and I have no desire to leave," she continued, with resolute determination.

The road from India's coral strand to the white cliffs of Dover had been a long and rough one. Little wonder, then, that the young Christian wanted to remain where she was settled and happy. Looking back through the years, she could almost hear the voice of her father, Rev. Nehemiah Goreh, telling her of the incidents surrounding her birth. "Your mother," he often reminded her, "was a high caste Brahmin. When I became a Christian, her parents were so enraged that they took her back home with them and refused to let me see her. But when her father died, some friends of mine went to her house and brought her out to the palki in which I sat waiting for her. Being near to me in the palki automatically broke her caste, according to the Indian beliefs of the day, and she went home with me. But," her father added, "she said she would never become a Christian. I didn't press the matter, but merely gave her some good books to read that awakened her interest in the new faith. Then you were born to us on September 11, 1853, and some weeks later your mother, Lakshmi, expressed the desire to be baptized with her new baby daughter. You were both dedicated to God in baptism on December 1, 1853, just three days before your mother died."

The road was a difficult one for the new baby after that. Her father, helpless and desolate, agreed to let her be adopted by an indigo planter and his wife. However, after five years, he lost all his property and then his life, in the Mutiny. The homeless little girl then was adopted for the second time by Rev. and Mrs. W. T. Storrs, a young missionary couple stationed at Benares, who had recently lost their first child. When they went to England on furlough several years later, they brought Ellen and their own children with them. When the Storrs returned to India, Ellen was adopted for the third time by Mr. Storrs' sister, who welcomed the gifted girl into her family that already included three boys and three girls. She was educated, meanwhile, in several English schools and was active in Sunday School and Church activities in many ways. At one time she taught a class of seventy mill girls who became very devoted to their "foreign" teacher.

It was several years after she had practically renounced her own people that God put these words in her heart. "You ought to be doing this among your own people." So she answered the call and prepared herself to be a Christian missionary. The next years saw her engaged in many varied activities. First, she taught in a girls' school at Amristar. Then she studied nursing and worked in a hospital in Allahabad. After that, she was elected Superintendent of the new Bishop Johnson Orphanage for Anglo-Indian children, serving in that capacity for nine years. She felt the call to become a Deaconess so she resigned from that responsible position and became a Deaconess, being ordained to that office in All Saints Cathedral, Allahabad, on St. Andrews' Day, 1897.

During her years in England she had begun to write poetry, an art she continued to practise as long as she lived. She remembered some remarks of England's leading woman hymn-writer, Frances Ridley Havergal, after reading some of her poems. Miss Havergal had said, "My candid opinion is that God has given you a real gift, which may be and ought to be used for His glory." Out of the busiest years of her life she wrote a beautiful hymn which revealed the secret of her unusual life. The first stanza contained these lines:

In the secret of His presence, How my soul delights to hide;
Oh, how precious are the lessons Which I learn at Jesus' side!
Earthly cares can never vex me, Neither trials lay me low;
For when Satan comes to tempt me, To the secret place I go.

Set to lovely music by George C. Stebbins sometime later, this hymn has won a permanent place in Christian hymnody.

In 1901, Ellen Goreh became associated with The Society for the Propagation of the Gospel, and laboured faithfully with its program until her retirement in 1919. She then did special work with Indian women in Kotgarh and Simla.

A young missionary who knew Miss Goreh's hymn was thrilled at the prospect of meeting her, though she was afraid the older woman would not come up to her expectations. But when she saw her she exclaimed, "Oh, she does do it. She does dwell in the secret place, and bear the image of the Master in her face." That glow was still there when Ellen entered St. Catherine's Hospital in Cawnpore in 1932. "I seem such a poor, weak, good-for-nothing little woman," she said. "I am in a very dilapitated condition, just waiting at the pearly gate until it is opened for me to enter."

Early in 1937, her eighty-fourth year, the gate was opened and she was welcomed home by Him who could well have said, "Well done, thou good and faithful servant; enter thou into the joy of thy Lord."

JESUS, LOVER OF MY SOUL

If Charles Wesley could have found a good one-syllable word to rhyme with "flee," his noblest hymn would not have achieved its universal popularity, and hymnologists would have been spared the ordeal of discounting many a romantic story about its origin. Finding no satisfactory word to meet his needs, Wesley wrote the first line to read, "Jesus, lover of my soul, Let me to thy bosom fly," thus giving rise to legends about a dove flying for protection into his bosom during a violent storm in rural England, and sea-gulls beating their wings at his porthole during tempests at sea, none of which contain even a grain of truth.

This eighteenth son of Samuel and Susanna Wesley did not pen these majestic lines until 1740, when he was thirty-three, the age at which his Lord had been crucified. It was four years after he had made the perilous journey across the Atlantic from Oglethorpe's colony in Georgia in the new world, and two years after his own heart had been "strangely warmed" on Whitsunday, May 20, 1738, "when he found peace with God and rejoiced in the hope of a living Christ."

However, his diary contains detailed accounts of several notable incidents that may have served as a background against which this hymn was ultimately written. His return trip to England across the ocean in 1738 had been anything but peaceful. The seas were far from tranquil and for days on end the passengers feared for their lives, as their vessel was tossed to and fro on the angry waves, at the mercy of the sea and the unpredictable whims of the wind and the tide. Charles had alternately prayed with excited passengers and for his own soul, while salty water poured into the hold in such quantities that, in spite of the fact that four men were pumping almost continually, the Captain ordered the mizzen mast cut to save the boat from sinking.

Half-alive as well as half-starved, the passengers finally

reached the shore in safety. Most of them immediately fell upon the ground in reverent prayer, offering their gratitude to God for having been spared from a watery grave. Such a harrowing experience is bound to leave its scars on any man's soul and Charles Wesley was no exception.

His interesting diary further records another unusual incident that occurred in 1738, in connection with his spiritual awakening. He had been suffering from a strange malady for several days during which he had been indisposed with what he thought was a combination of pleurisy and dysentery. Suddenly one afternoon he thought he saw a woman he knew entering his room and walking over to stand beside his bed. While he stared at the apparition in amazement, she said, "In the name of Jesus of Nazareth, arise and believe and thou shalt be healed." When the vision faded, the sick man leaped from his bed and ran downstairs looking for the woman, but she was nowhere to be found. Turning to the Bible, he consoled himself with God's "exceeding great and precious promises," and then realized that his bodily strength was returning and that he was getting well. Such a dramatic and unexpected episode will be remembered in detail as long as one lives and Wesley was no exception.

His third experience had to do with the conversion of several condemned criminals, with whom he spent many hours prior to their execution by hanging in July of that same year. He had the joy of ushering several of these felons into the Kingdom of God just before their death, and thus realized afresh the power of the Gospel to save to the uttermost even those in the very depths of despair.

These unforgettable experiences formed the background against which the "sweet singer of Methodism" was inspired to write one of the noblest hymns in all literature.

Of the more than six thousand hymns Charles Wesley penned during his long and fruitful life, 1707-1788, this is by far the most outstanding. Since it was written before Wesleyan sermons incited mobs to riot and crowds to assault the brother preachers, the story that Wesley wrote the stanzas while hiding from ruffians in a farmer's milk-house is as legendary as the dove and sea-gull tales.

As for the tune "Martyn," to which these stanzas are sung, it was not composed for Wesley's lines at all. Simeon Marsh wrote the music for John Newton's hymn, "Mary, at her Saviour's tomb," about one hundred years after Wesley had fashioned his famous lines. It was Thomas Hastings, composer of the tune "Toplady" to which "Rock of Ages" is sung, who wedded Marsh's music and Wesley's words and set "Jesus, lover of my soul," singing its way into immortality.

JESUS, TENDER SHEPHERD, HEAR ME

"Mrs. William Wallace Duncan," the young bride said. "I'll have to get used to that name, darling."

"It's not a bad name, is it?" he asked.

"I like it," she replied, "although I never could see why a girl had to give up her name entirely when she took unto herself a husband. There ought to be some way to equalize this business of who takes whose name."

"For instance?" he asked.

"Well," she replied, "some old English families were so proud of their names that the bride took the groom's name and the groom took the bride's, and that's where so many of these long, hyphenated names came from, like Baring-Gould, and others."

"The best way to handle that," he answered, "would be for me to take your last name, Lundie, and let you take my last name, Duncan; in that way I would become Mr. William Lundie Duncan and you would be known as Mrs. William Lundie Duncan. Personally, I think that would be terrible."

"And I agree with you, William. I'll settle for Mrs. William Wallace Duncan," she said, as she put her arms lovingly about him, "and I hope to be able to wear that name for a long, long time," she added, the week following their wedding on July 11, 1836. "I am glad of one thing, though," she said.

"What is that?" he asked.

"That your name, Duncan, didn't come from the Scottish king, Duncan, who was murdered by Macbeth."

"Heaven forbid!" he shouted. "He may be the black sheep in the family, but he's no relative of mine, thank goodness. If you want to claim kinship with any distinguished Duncans, then hold on to my father's name!" he said, proudly.

"That I will, dear. He has already given your name great honor, and I know that you will add more lustre to it in the years that are ahead," she continued.

Her husband's father, Rev. Henry Duncan, of Ruthwell, was honored as The Inventor of the Savings Bank, no small distinction for a minister who invades the world of high finance, despite the fact that some scholars divide the credit for this undertaking between Daniel Defoe, author of "Robinson Crusoe," who suggested it in 1697, and the Savings Bank that opened in Brunswick, Germany, in 1765. But, since the wife of a minister rarely has enough money to place in a savings account, Mary Lundie Duncan basked in the reflected glory of her father-in-law's economic genius, and devoted all of her time to the task of being a good wife and a devoted mother.

Her father, Rev. Robert Lundie, of Kelso, Scotland, had had his talented daughter educated in London, since she had shown an unusual aptitude for writing poetry at an early age, and had constantly encouraged her to develop her gifts since they had been given to her in trust by her Heavenly Father. Since devotion to the Christian ministry flowed in her father's veins, it was not unusual that one daughter became the wife of Rev. William Duncan and the other married Rev. Horatius Bonar, preacher, author, poet and hymn writer. In the latter marriage, the husband outshone his wife, while in the former, the talented wife outshone her husband. During the Duncans' stay at Cleish, Kinross-shire, his first pastoral charge, two precious children were born to their family, and the unusually beautiful and accomplished woman whom the pastor had taken for his bride, revealed herself an equally faithful and devoted mother.

"I never could understand why Jesus said, 'Suffer the little children to come unto me,' she said to him one evening as they were visiting before retiring, "until I discovered that the English language has changed immensely in the centuries since the Authorized Version of 1611 was published. Some people are so ignorant that they refuse to take their sick children to doctors, on the grounds that Jesus said 'Suffer the little children.' Could anything be more horrible than to misuse the Bible in that way?"

Her husband nodded his agreement, as she continued, "Then, when I learned from a study of the original Greek that Jesus was actually saying, 'Let the children alone so they may come unto me,' or 'Let the children alone and they will come unto me,' I felt better about it. It sounded more like the Jesus I love and more like the God He revealed."

"When one has children, he begins to see things in such a different light," her husband added. "The experience of being a father gives one insights into the Fatherhood of God that you can't get from books."

"Did I tell you that I was writing some poems for our own two children, darling?" she asked him.

"For our children? Why, Mary, they're too small to understand."

"I know they are tiny babies, dear, but I just felt it in my heart to write some simple little prayers that they could learn when they grew up," his wife explained, "and it seemed so natural for a mother to want to write prayers for her little ones, so they could learn to know that God loves them and that Jesus, the Good Shepherd, is interested in them always."

"Let me hear one of them, Mary," he said.

"I wrote this one the other afternoon after the baby fell asleep. She looked so angelic lying there, that the words came out, almost without conscious effort.

Jesus, tender shepherd, hear me, Bless thy little lamb tonight; Through the darkness be thou near me, Keep me safe till morning light."

When she finished the third stanza, her husband took her in his arms. "God has given you so many talents, Mary, so many wonderful gifts," he said, lovingly, "and the best of all is that I love you and you love me with a deathless and an undying love."

Tragically, after only three and a half years of happy wedded bliss, the kind that some people experience only in the pages of a book, but which had been theirs in day to day living, Mary Duncan took pneumonia, and died suddenly, at the age of twenty-six, January 5, 1840. Her mother gathered up twenty-three of her daughter's poems, written between July and December of 1839 for her own two tiny children, and published them the year of Mary's death. Two years later, these gems were included in a volume entitled "Rhymes for My Children."

Though she died so young, Mary Lundie Duncan, by means

of her poetic prayers, has made it easier for millions of other little children to become devout Christians, for her verses say what she wanted the Scripture, correctly translated, to say to them, "Let the children alone that they may come unto me, for of such is the Kingdom of Heaven."

JOY TO THE WORLD

Competition may be stimulating, but controversy is destructive. The British impressario, D'Oyly Carte, pitted librettist W. S. Gilbert against composer Arthur Sullivan, with the result that each man worked himself to the bone to outdo the other in producing the famous Gilbert and Sullivan light operas, but the damage to their friendship was irreparable.

Another famous stage controversy that came to an equally fatal end involved the two most renowned operatic composers of the eighteenth century, Handel and Bononcini. The two talented men went at it so hard and heavy to prove to the fickle public which one was the master of the field that both of them collapsed, physically as well as financially, in 1737. In addition to being forced to take out bankruptcy, Handel suffered a partial stroke which left his health shattered for months.

John Byrom, author of the Christmas hymn, "Christians, Awake, salute the happy morn," poked fun at the two composers in an oft-quoted verse:

Some say, compared to Bononcini, That Mynheer Handel's but
    a ninny;
Others aver that he to Handel, Is scarcely fit to hold a candle.
Strange all this difference should be,
Twixt Tweedledum and Tweedledee!

This was neither the first nor the last time that German-born George Frederick Handel had become involved in such a situation. His father had insisted that the lad follow the legal profession, while young George was equally insistent that he wanted to pursue a musical career. Fortunately, or unfortunately, the conflict was resolved when the senior Handel died, whereupon the younger Handel left the law school of the University of Halle and concentrated upon his musical studies. By the time he reached his teens, he had mastered nearly every orchestral instrument, and before he was twenty, he had written enough music to do honor to a composer three times his age.

His next involvement came after he had successfully served as the choirmaster of the Elector of Hanover, and asked for a leave of absence in which to travel. When he arrived in England, his music was greeted so enthusiastically and he was so lionized by the populace that he decided to move from Hanover to the island kingdom. This did not increase his popularity with his former patron, but Handel let bygones be bygones and began to build for himself a new reputation in his adopted country. However, fate has a way of playing cruel jokes on the innocent and guilty alike, and, to his shock and surprise, Handel learned one day that his former benefactor, The Elector of Hanover, was coming to London in 1714 as King George I of England. He quickly conquered his fears and composed his brilliant "Water Music" which is said to have re-established him in the favor of the royal family.

The next few years were as peaceable as a musician who courts popular favor can expect, what with composing operas and being the figure the public expects you to portray. But the peace and quiet were too good to be true, and the next controversy broke when Handel hinted that he was writing a new opera based upon the life of the Biblical heroine, Queen Esther. The Bishop of London fussed and fumed. "What are we coming to?" he asked, "when the will of Satan is imposed upon us in this fashion—putting Biblical characters on the iniquitous stage?"

But Handel was equal to the situation, and put Esther on the stage, minus backdrops and costumed characters and violent action, but with all the music by chorus and soloists as he wrote it to be sung, and thus the first oratorio was born. The Royal Family liked it, and Handel discovered the finest medium for his versatile talents after he had reached what his critics caustically called "his zenith."

Unlike Mozart, Handel never starved. If the royalty that supported him and paid the bills liked a certain style, he "went to town" in that style with an enthusiasm that brooked no opposition and ignored all criticism. Benefit concerts were always certain to raise sufficient funds to "bail him out of bankruptcy" and several times he called upon the public and they rallied to his support.

His most remarkable composition was penned in just twenty-four days in the year 1741, when the composer was fifty-six years old. Entitled "The Messiah," it was first sung in the English language before an Irish audience in Dublin, with the German-born composer conducting, on April 13, 1742. Those who heard the closing glory of "The Hallelujah Chorus" could well believe the composer's words after he had written it, for he had said, "I did think I did see all Heaven before me and the Great God Himself." And they rose and stood in reverent tribute to the genius who produced it, until the last echo of the last "Hallelujah" died away in the distance.

Handel expressed the desire to die on Good Friday, and God must have heard his prayer, because on Good Friday, April 13, 1759, seven days after he had attended his last performance of his grandest work, he died, in his seventy-fourth year.

Themes from his masterpiece have been arranged and rearranged times without number. One theme, coupled with Isaac Watts' free rendition of Psalm 98, first published in 1719, comprises one of our finest Advent hymns, "Joy to the world, the Lord is come." Another theme, taken from his opera "Siroe" composed in 1728, is the now familiar hymn tune "Christmas" to which "While shepherds watched their flocks by night" is universally sung. His stately "Largo" from the opera "Xerxes" has long since been accorded a place worthy of its dignity in the preludes and postludes of public worship.

This fluent and voluminous composer was buried in Westminster Abbey, but he lives on in the music which poured from heaven through him to brighten, beautify and inspire God's children the world over. Someone has aptly said, "Bach's 'Passion' is a religious service, but Handel's 'Messiah' is a sermon." A more eloquent one would be hard to find.

LOOK, YE SAINTS, THE SIGHT
IS GLORIOUS

To the average school child, the "Three Rs" refer to education and stand for "reading, 'riting and 'rithmetic." But to Irishman Thomas Kelly (1769-1854) they referred to matrimony and stood for a wife who was "romantic, rich and reasonable." She was romantic because she fell in love with him at the same time that he had the good fortune to fall in love with her; rich, because she had inherited considerable property, which meant that if he were ever put out of the Church for the fervent fire of his evangelistic preaching, he could erect his own houses of worship and preach what and to whom he pleased; and reasonable, because she had the good sense to see that her views in theological matters were similar to his own. Consequently a more ideal marriage would be hard to find.

His courtship was quite a contrast to that of another hymn writer and distinguished Church leader, Count Zinzindorf. Some seventy-six years before Kelly found his ideal mate, Nicholas Lewis, Count and Lord of Zinzindorf, fell in love with the Countess Theodora of Castel. To his dismay, he learned that the mother of his intimate friend, Count Reuss, had already picked out the charming young lady for her own son. With typical German resignation to parental authority, he relinquished his claim upon her, and courted his rival's sister, marrying her and living happily ever after. Of Zinzindorf's two thousand hymns written during the first half of the eighteenth century, the one translated "Jesus, still lead on" alone has found a permanent place in English and American hymnody. In contrast, of the more than seven hundred hymns that Thomas Kelly wrote over a similar fifty-year period, spanning the first half of the nineteenth century, at least three are in general use in English speaking countries.

Kelly, born appropriately in a place called Kellyville, in County Queens, Ireland, was, like John Wesley, unusually well trained in the finest preparatory schools and universities of his day. Although he originally intended to become a lawyer, a study of the Hebrew language led him to inquire further into the Bible, as a result of which he became an ardent student of religion and Christianity in particular. For a while he struggled as hard to become worthy of his salvation as had John Wesley before him. But, while Wesley's change was due to an experience when he felt his heart "strangely warmed," Kelly's was a change of attitude, similar to that of Martin Luther, when he discovered the doctrine of "justification by faith" in the Holy Scripture. Giving up his former ascetic ways, by which he had hoped to earn divine favor and the blessings of salvation, he began to preach with such evangelical fervor that Archbishop Fowler of Dublin closed the pulpits of the Established Churches to him and his clergyman friend, Rowland Hill.

"Wesley stepped outside the Church door and stood on the marble slab over his father's grave and preached to the multitudes when the pulpits of England were closed to him," Kelly said to Hill. "But since I am no Wesley, I will go him one better, and hire a hall where people can gather and hear me preach."

"The Archbishop will do what he can to keep his people from hearing you," Hill warned. "He may even tell the Anglicans that you are committing a sin by preaching in an unconsecrated building."

Kelly laughed. "I've had enough of that foolishness," he replied. "No form of worship or liturgical ceremony can make a building any more or less holy than the hearts of those who preach and listen inside its walls. If there ever was an unconsecrated piece of ground it was that spot on the plain of Midian where Moses saw the burning bush. Since then, wherever God meets man or man meets God, that place is holy ground, whether the Archbishop recognizes that fact or not."

Hill nodded. "God looks with favor upon apostolic success," he said, "while the Church places its primary emphasis upon apostolic succession."

"Well said," Kelly replied. But the pressure was on, and it was

101

not long before Kelly withdrew entirely from the Established Church of England and preached in several Churches which he himself built with his wife's money, and where those who wished could come and hear sermons delivered by one who preached without fear or favor.

"If the rector of St. Luke's in Dublin regards my messages as too spiritual," the talented pastor said, "then Luke himself would not be welcome within those stiff and stately walls. Because he was as evangelistic as they come. If you don't believe me, read the fifteenth chapter of his gospel, the three parables of things lost, and re-read the Parable of the Good Samaritan. If I am too warm-hearted a preacher, so was he; and if he was too enthusiastic an evangelist, so was his Lord!"

In the third edition of the author's book, "Hymns on Various Passages of Scripture," published in 1809, his majestic masterpiece, "Look ye saints, the sight is glorious, See the man of sorrows now, From the fight returned victorious, Every knee to him shall bow," appeared in print for the first time. The second edition, published three years earlier, had included his popular hymn "Hark, ten thousand harps and voices." But "Look ye saints," based upon Revelation 11:15, 'The kingdoms of this world are become the kingdoms of our Lord and of his Christ; and he shall reign forever and ever,' and equal to the finest of Watts and Wesley, was inspired by the same Scripture verse which moved Handel to compose his immortal "Hallelujah Chorus."

The 1820 edition of this same volume included another gem, "The head that once was crowned with thorns, Is crowned with glory now." Kelly, a gifted musician as well as poet, even wrote tunes for many of his hymns, and was so versatile that he penned his poems in many different metrical patterns. When he was eight-four, he brought out the final edition of his "Hymns," prefacing it with these words, "Though there is an interval between the first and last (edition) of nearly sixty years, both speak of the same great truths in the same way. Nothing that (the author) has seen or heard has made the least change in his mind as to the grand truths of the Gospel."

At eighty-six, as he lay on his deathbed, a friend sought to comfort him by reading the Twenty-third Psalm. He began slowly, "The Lord is my shepherd" only to have the aged clergyman cry out, "The Lord is my everything." Then, with the prayer, "Not my will but thine be done," he went home to give his heavenly Father an accounting of his stewardship. He who had sung of his Lord in his grandest hymn, "Crowns become the victor's brow," surely must have received from the Master's hand "a crown of glory" which had been laid up for him against that day.

NOW I LAY ME DOWN TO SLEEP

"What did you say the new president's name was?" a freshman at Hamilton College, New York, asked an upper classman one September afternoon in 1892.

"Rev. Dr. Melanchthon Woolsey Stryker," replied the older student.

"Boy, what a mouthful!" the freshman said. "Where did his parents ever dig up a name like that?"

"Well, you know who Melanchthon was, don't you?" the upper classman asked.

"Never heard of him," the freshman replied. "Who was he anyway?"

"You'll find out before you finish freshman history, if I know the professor like I think I do. He'll ring the changes on the Renaissance and the Reformation. And when you study the Reformation he'll have you reading reams of parallel on Martin Luther and his right-hand man, Philipp Melanchthon (1497-1560)."

"How come you remember those dates?"

"Either remember them or you'll flunk out," the wiser upper classman counselled. "Melanchthon was a professor of Greek New Testament at Wittenberg, Germany, and a close friend and co-worker of Luther. In fact, he was more of a mediator than the great Martin, and held some of the hostile forces of the Reformation together while the new movement developed strength. He shaped up Luther's theology like John Calvin shaped up the theology of the Reformed Churches, and was generally regarded as the ablest theologian in the early years of the Lutheran movement."

"So the new president is a theologian, is that it?" the young student asked.

"Not exactly," his counsellor explained, "but he is a clergyman, if that is what you are wondering about. He served several Presbyterian churches after he graduated from Hamilton and from Auburn Seminary, and then accepted a call to serve the Second Congregational Church at Holyoke, Massachusetts. But he comes to his Alma Mater from the Fourth Presbyterian Church in Chicago where he has been pastor for the past seven years."

"He really gets around, doesn't he?" the freshman asked.

"He is not only a distinguished preacher," the older youth explained, "but also something of a writer and a poet. He has written several hymns and sacred poems and I understand he has also edited a hymnal or two."

"What about his middle name? You forgot to tell me where the 'Woolsey' came from?"

"Some of us thought that he was named for Cardinal Wolsey who lived back in the days when Henry VIII of England broke with the Pope of Rome and set up the Anglican Church with himself at the head. But the Cardinal was a Catholic and spelled his name with one 'o' while President Stryker spells his with two. We discovered that it was his mother's maiden name before her marriage to his father, Rev. Isaac Stryker."

"Well, thanks for the information. I'll pass it on to the other freshmen like I was a member of the family," the younger student added as he walked over to inspect the college library nearby.

The older student was correct in stating that the new president had written hymns and edited hymnals. In fact, as early as 1882, his thirty-first year, he had collaborated with Hubert P. Main in bringing out "The Church Praise Book." "Hymns and Verses" followed the very next year, and "Christian Chorals" in 1885. While serving the large Chicago Church, he had worked lovingly and long on a new volume, "Church Song," which was published in 1889, three years before he left the active pastorate for the duties of a College president. For this new volume he wrote hymns on a wide variety of subjects, in a tone that was dogmatic and fiery, but in a style that sometimes lacked unity and purity of rhythm. There were quite a few hymns on Christian Missions, several National Hymns, some for the administering of the Sacraments as well as for funerals, and others designed to be sung on Trinity Sunday,

Easter, on the occasion of the opening of a new Church and on miscellaneous general subjects as well.

"Watts tried his hand at writing verses for children," he said to a friend one day when he was at work on some material for the forth-coming volume, "but he talked down to the children. That is one thing a poet must never do. He has to write on the children's level without appearing to be condescending or without trying too hard to get down to where the child is. For example, many generations were raised on Watts' verses about dogs and bees. They are all right, but when he began to moralize and draw lessons, he overstepped his bounds. Listen to this:

Let dogs delight to bark and bite, For God hath made them so.

If he had stopped there, I would have no quarrel with him. But he didn't. He went on to add:

But, children, you should never let, Such angry passions rise; Your little hands were never made To tear each other's eyes.

When he said that, he ruined it all, as far as I'm concerned."

"If I recall correctly," his friend said, "Watts wrote his hymns because he objected to those that were being used in his day."

"That's right," the minister agreed.

"And he wrote 'Behold, the glories of the Lamb,' when his father told him that he should not criticize the hymns being used unless he could do better."

"Right, again," Stryker said. Then, looking up with a smile, he added, "Are you suggesting that I have no right to criticize Watts unless I can do better?"

His friend laughed. "Draw your own conclusions," he replied.

Stryker picked up a piece of paper from his desk and said, "I have a simple poem that I call 'Child's Evening Hymn.' I wrote it back in 1884, and plan to include it in 'Church Song.' In fact, according to my calculations, it will be Number 513 in the new volume. Want to hear it?"

"Of course," his friend said.

Stryker read as follows:

106

Now I lay me down to sleep; I pray the Lord my soul to keep.
If I should die before I wake, I pray the Lord my soul to take.

"Isn't that last line a bit morbid, that part about dying?" his friend asked.

"Why should it be?" the minister replied. "The only way we can come into the world is by the miracle of birth and the only way we can leave it is by the miracle of death. Children should be taught that death is as much a part of God's plan as birth. To ignore death or try to misinterpret it is morbid. To face it and accept it as a Christian is to act wisely and intelligently," he added.

Of all the poems in the 1889 edition of "Church Song," this is the only one that has outlived its day, and, while numerous substitutes have been suggested during the intervening years, none has supplanted it as the favorite of children the world over.

Stryker authored and edited many volumes before his death in 1929 at the age of seventy-eight, but, while he is remembered as the author of the hymn "Almighty God, with one accord, We offer Thee our youth," written in 1896, he is loved as the forgotten author of the four-line children's prayer, which begins, "Now I lay me down to sleep."

NOW THANK WE ALL OUR GOD

"We must now bury the dead in trenches," Bishop Martin Rinkhart said to his pastors in Eilenberg, Germany. "For days now we have been burying them in separate graves—first by the tens and then by the scores. Now there is neither room for their graves nor men strong enough to dig them and cover them up again." The clergymen nodded understandingly. "Eilenberg is the last city of refuge left. We may expect more and more refugees in the weeks ahead. The war will not subside, but will be pressed by the enemy until the last man of us takes his place in some trench alongside those already lying there, stiff and cold in death," the Bishop continued. "But we will not surrender! As God is our helper, we will not give in!"

"Bishop," one of the pastors said, "our people are already starving. Where are we to find food for the others who are expected?"

"In my parish," another minister explained, "the people are already fighting over scraps of stale bread."

"And in mine," a third interrupted, "they are reduced to quarreling over the bodies of dead birds, and men kill their neighbours over the carcass of a dead dog, or the skeletal remains of an alley cat."

"And after that," the Bishop said solemnly, "will come the plague. The four horsemen are riding again: the white horse of conquest, the red horse of war, the black horse of famine and pestilence and the pale horse of death! We must commit ourselves into the hands of God, who alone can save us in this dark and dreadful hour."

The ministers then engaged in a period of fervent prayer, after which each man returned to his respective parish, wondering which of them would be alive when they gathered together a few days hence in the Bishop's study, adjoining the cathedral. The Thirty Years War had been waged back and forth across

108

that part of Germany for more than a quarter of a century. The fields, once rich with ripening grain, were now soggy with the blood of those slain upon the altars of Moloch, and offered up as living sacrifices to satisfy the insatiable hunger of Mars, the god of war! To heap cruelty upon cruelty, the victorious invading armies successively quartered their troops in the homes of the citizens of the city.

"I do my share of soul-searching," Rinkhart told one of his intimate friends, "for in my home, too, the enemy has quartered his soldiers. With one hand I want to destroy them, and yet, with the other, I struggle to obey the words of the Lord, 'Love your enemies,' and the admonition of St. Paul, 'Vengeance is mine, I will repay, saith the Lord; so if thine enemy hunger, feed him; if he thirst, give him drink.' Yet it is not easy, my friend."

"Nor was the Master's cross," his friend reminded him.

"Last year," the Bishop continued, "we buried eight thousand. What will it be this year? Last year men fought for crumbs. What will they fight over this year? The bodies of their unborn or still-born children? Will we see a recurrence of those horrible days described by Josephus, when the Romans under Titus laid siege to Jerusalem, captured the city and laid it waste? Those days when women slew women over the bodies of their dead and dying infants? Will we come to that?" he shouted.

The next months were strenuous ones, as the pastors gave themselves unselfishly to the service of God and their fellow men. They comforted the dying, fed the starving, cheered the desperate, buried the dead, gave hope to the depressed and strength to the tempted. Then the Swedish army swept through the city once again, driving out the forces that had sought refuge within her walls, and the General, to punish the inhabitants for not welcoming him and his men with open arms, promptly and arrogantly ordered the citizens to pay him tribute equal to $25,000 in cash. Rinkhart gathered his ministers and people about him and said, "We have no money, nor have we any jewels or precious stones. We cannot pay what is demanded of us. So let us go together, in the power of God, to intercede before the General of the Swedish Army."

They marched through the gates of the city and stood defiantly before the tent-headquarters of the foreign commander. Rinkhart explained to the General the condition of the city and its inhabitants.

"We are willing to meet your demands," he said, "but we do not have that with which to meet them."

The people fell on their knees as Rinkhart pleaded on their behalf, but to no avail. When the military leader rejected their appeal, the Bishop turned to his people and said, "Come, my children, we can find no mercy with men; let us turn to God." And there on the plain before their ruined city, he lifted up his heart and voice to God with such feeling and power that the General, seeking refuge in his tent, could not escape his words nor the emotion with which he spoke. Throwing back the tent flaps, he called out to Rinkhart, "Pay me $1,500 and be done with you!" As he stormed back to review plans for further military operations, the Bishop slowly rose from his knees, motioned to his people, who also got to their feet, and the pathetic army of the faithful slowly and proudly returned to Eilenberg.

Sacked once by the Austrians and twice by the Swedes, the people had little left. Nevertheless they scraped together the demanded tribute, which Rinkhart personally delivered to the conqueror. Meanwhile, he had mortgaged himself for years to come in order to purchase scraps of food for the starving and clothing for the naked. Despite the pressures under which he lived and worked, he found time to write several stirring dramas of the Reformation as well as numerous other literary works. In addition, he penned sixty-six hymns before wearing himself out and dying at sixty-three, in 1649. This prolific writer and brilliant musician and composer, in gratitude to God for the final conclusion of the gory conflict which had been waged in and about his city, recalling the words of St. Paul, 'In everything give thanks' and the admonition found in Ecclesiastes, 'And now let all praise God who hath done great things,' wrote his immortal hymn, 'Nun danket alle Gott.' As translated by Catherine Winkworth in 1858, his first stanza reads as follows:

Now thank we all our God, With hearts and hands and voices;
Who wondrous things hath done, In whom his world rejoices;
Who from our mother's arms, Hath led us on our way
With countless gifts of love, And still is ours today.

The passing of centuries only enhances the glory and grandeur
of these autobiographical lines, and reminds successive generations of Christians that 'In everything, God works for good
with those who love him.'

O GOD OUR HELP IN AGES PAST

Isaac Watts was a peace loving little man and would have been horrified had he known that some of his hymns were to play a prominent part in the American Revolutionary War.

While he was a religious and ecclesiastical non-conformist, his spirit of dissent did not carry over into the political field and he was content to alter the singing habits of Christendom all by himself, leaving the banners of state to be carried by stronger and more capable hands.

In his day, Watts, (1674-1748), deplored the poor condition of congregational singing and blamed it as much on the lack of hymns good enough to be sung as upon the indolent clergy who relegated the musical portions of public worship to the paid choir and organist. "God stopped speaking in poetic meters when David died," he was often told by those who felt it their bounden duty to discourage him from writing original hymns for use by his fellow non-conformists. But Watts knew more about God than did his critics, and refused to hearken to their gloomy voices of doom. The beauty of his soul and brilliant clarity of his mind seemed to be in direct contrast to his outward appearance. The only woman he ever loved took but one look at him and said, "I'm sorry, Dr. Watts," and that was as close as he ever came to committing matrimony. But they remained good friends for many years, for she later softened the blow of her blunt refusal by adding, "I admired the jewel but not the casket."

Saul, the first King of Israel, was a head taller than most men of his day, but his heart was in the gutter much of the time. Watts, on the other hand, stood a mere five feet tall, but was blest with a heart that communed with the Infinite and made the living God a reality to the believers of his day. He lacked the handsome figure and face of Absalom, because his large nose, low forehead, prominent cheek bones and small piercing grey eyes neither drew a second glance from admirers of physical perfection nor ever caused a maiden's heart to skip a beat when he walked by. But the shining beauty of his real self illumines the pages of his many books and causes the light of God as revealed in the face of Jesus Christ to shine with added lustre upon the children of men.

Wholly dedicating himself to the task of revolutionizing the hymnodic habits of his day, he began by versifying the revered Psalms of David, in order to convince his opponents that he had no ulterior motive in view other than giving the Christians of the day better hymns by means of which to praise their God. His first volume was published in 1706, followed by another the very next year. Both of these books went through several editions, even as he was preparing additional manuscripts for the publishers. In 1715 his hymns and poems for children was released, and in 1719, his monumental work, "The Psalms of David, Imitated" came from the press. In this book there appeared for the first time his majestic poem, "Our God, Our Help In Ages Past." It was inspired by Psalm 90, "Lord, thou hast been our dwelling place in all generations," and was printed under the caption "Man Frail and God Eternal." John Wesley, the founder of the Methodist Church, later changed the first word from "Our" to "O," and the hymn appears under either or both of these titles in most hymnals in the English speaking world.

Men of letters paid the author a high tribute by stating that his writing of this hymn alone was enough to insure him a permanent place in the hearts of the British people. The very nobility of his writings soon disposed of his critics and he lived to see his works accepted enthusiastically by a grateful people.

A quarter of a century after his death, the thirteen colonies that comprised the United States of America went to war against Great Britain for freedom and independence. The conflict was a long, gruelling and bloody one. Among the many battles fought between the poorly-equipped forces under General Washington and the well-trained mercenaries from across the Atlantic was a rather insignificant one known as "The Battle of Springfield." The Rev. James Caldwell was pastor of the Presbyterian Church in Elizabeth, New Jersey, in May,

1780, when the British forces sallied forth from their head-quarters at Staten Island and burned the nearby town of Spring-field. The pastor's wife was one of the casualties of the raid. Three weeks later, in June, when the enemy attempted a repitition of this action, Washington's militia was on the ground, all lined up to give them battle. Suddenly the defenders discovered that there was a tragic and almost fatal shortage of wadding for their guns. When the minister heard the news, he rushed back to his Church, picked up an armful of hymnals and hurried back to the scene of battle. Handing the books to the fighters up and down the line, he cried out, "Give 'em Watts, boys! Give 'em Watts!" The desperate soldiers tore out the pages of the books and gave the enemy what their Chaplain had commanded. In a quarter of a century the hymns of the English divine had found such a place in the worship of the free Churches that his name was synonymous with the hymnbook! What higher tribute could any hymn writer gain in so short a period of time!

This act was in keeping with American ingenuity, however, because, a few months earlier, some of the lead pipes from the large pipe organ in Christ Church, Cambridge, Massachusetts, had been melted down to make bullets for the Battle of Bunker Hill. Ironically, the instrument had been secured through the good graces of the Lord Mayor of London in 1764.

Be that as it may, today the hymns of Watts and the pipe organs that grace our Churches serve as another bond of unity between the independent Republic on one side of the Atlantic and the Mother country on the other.

O HAPPY DAY THAT FIXED MY CHOICE

When Rev. Robert Lowry added the words and music of a "Chorus" to Mrs. Annie Hawks' poem "I need thee every hour," he improved her hymn immeasurably, as did William Bradbury when he composed the musical setting for "He leadeth me, O blessed thought." But when Lowry did the same thing for Isaac Watts' "Come we that love the Lord" and transformed the stately hymn into the lilting strains of "We're marching to Zion," he detracted from the majesty and dignity of Watts' heroic stanzas which had been sung to the cadences of the tune "St. Thomas" for over a hundred years. Later R. E. Hudson did a similar thing with Watts' "Alas and did my Saviour bleed," in composing the gospel song known as "At the cross."

The hymns of Philip Doddridge (1702-1751) were subjected to a like fate, and, to this day, it is a matter of conjecture and debate whether the addition of a "Chorus" has added to or taken from their effectiveness. The hymn that illustrates this fact is his most popular one, "O happy day that fixed my choice, On thee, my Saviour and my God; Well may this glowing heart rejoice And tell its raptures all abroad." The stanzas first appeared in Mr. Orton's posthumous edition of the poet-preacher's "Hymns," brought out in 1755, four years after Doddridge's death in Lisbon, Portugal, where he had gone in search of a better climate to alleviate the sufferings of tuberculosis. Published under the title, "Rejoicing in our covenant engagements to God," the hymn was based upon II Chronicles 15:5, "And all Judaea rejoiced at the oath; for they had sworn with all their heart, and sought him with their whole desire; and he was found of them; and the Lord gave them rest round about." Sung to any standard Long Meter tune (one composed for a poem written in four lines with eight syllables in each line), it was quickly picked up by the English people and recognized as one of the author's noblest hymns. Queen Victoria's husband held it in such high regard that he had it sung at the confirmation of their children, a fitting tribute to the poet, who himself had been the twentieth child of a successful London merchant father and a staunch and devout Bohemian Lutheran mother.

For the next century, "O Happy Day" appeared in the major hymnals of the Churches and was sung to the dignified Long Meter tunes which were dear to the hearts of the people. Meanwhile, a distinguished English composer, Edward Francis Rimbault (1816-1876) had made a name for himself not only as a brilliant organist but also as a composer, author, editor and lecturer. His fame had spread to the United States, where Harvard University conferred upon him the honorary LL.D. degree and offered him the Professorship of Music. He accepted the degree but declined the offer. The third edition of Baker's "Biographical Dictionary of Musicians," awarded him a full page (two columns), which attests to his ability and accomplishments. Of his numerous and voluminous works, one simple song, "Happy Land" caught the public's fancy, and, after his books, cantatas, anthems and miscellaneous works were forgotten, the people were still singing the lilting refrain, "Happy land, Happy land! Whate'er my fate in life may be."

In the United States, the evangelistic fervor of the pioneer preachers had established the Camp Meeting as a vital factor in the nation's religious and social life. Already, the Americans were creating their own distinctive type of religious music, and adapting the hymns of other years to their own spiritual needs. Such early American melodies as "Amazing Grace," "Contrast" (How tedious and tasteless the hours) and "The Lily of the Valley" were increasingly popular. It was about this time, during the middle of the nineteenth century, that a member of the Maine Conference of the Methodist Church, Rev. Mr. McDonald, published a book entitled "The Wesleyan Sacred Harp," dated Boston, 1854. In its pages was found an adaptation of Dr. Rimbault's popular ditty "Happy Land" for the stanzas of Doddridge's hymn "O Happy Day," with a chorus thrown in for good measure. It was not long before the revivalists were singing, "Happy day, happy day, When Jesus washed my sins away," attributed to Doddridge who had never said any such thing. But the new music, while detracting from the effectiveness of the stanzas in some circles, certainly made them better known in others. However, a tune that can be taken from a song and made into a hymn can just as easily become a song again, and that was the final step in the "degradation" of "Happy land."

When my brother was Minister of Music in a Baptist Church in New England, it was the custom of the pastor to tell the children a story during the first part of the morning service. At the close of his narrative, the organist would play a tune that fitted the moral of the story, while the children left the Sanctuary for an extended session in their classrooms. One Sunday, the minister told of the days when the earth was cursed with an extended drought. He pictured the animals and people searching for water as the sun dried up the wells and creeks and rivers, and he vividly portrayed the way some of them died of thirst on the dusty plains and on the hot sands of the deserts. Finally, God sent the gift of rain, for which everyone was glad and rejoiced. The moral was, of course, "Thank God for the gift of rain." Brother wondered what piece of music would be appropriate as the children marched out that morning, since he wouldn't dare play the popular songs "Rain" or "I get the blues when it rains." After thinking seriously about the matter, he said to himself, "I have it. Rain washes and cleanses. So I'll play the hymn that says 'When Jesus washed my sins away.' " As the children left the auditorium that morning he began to play the hymn "O Happy Day," to the consternation of the congregation, many of whom later accused him of playing, "Nobody knows how dry I am!"

Fortunately Rimbault was spared the shock of knowing that the convivial imbibers had taken "O Happy Day" from "Happy Land" and made it the final shame of the dismal drunk! Whether the tune will live on as "Happy Day" or "Nobody Knows," remains to be seen. But of Rev. Philip Doddridge's more than four-hundred hymns, "Awake my soul, stretch every nerve," "Great God we sing thy mighty hand," "How pleasant God's commands," "See Israel's gentle shepherd stand," "My gracious Lord, I own thy right," "Let Zion's watchmen all awake," and "The King of heaven his table spreads" are all in common usage today, but not one has been as badly treated or is as well known as "O Happy Day."

O JESUS I HAVE PROMISED

"What is the Church?" Rev. John Ernest Bode asked his children. "Is it a building?"

"No," answered his eldest son. "The Church is first of all a group of people. After the people get together they build the building."

"That's right, son," his fifty-year-old minister father replied. "Now what else is the Church, in addition to being a group of people? Or what distinguishes this group of people from any other?"

His youngest daughter spoke up. "I know, father. The Church is a group of people who gather together to worship God."

"Exactly," he replied. "Can you be a Christian if you refuse to gather together with other Christians?"

"Yes, daddy," the second daughter replied, "but not a very good one. God expects his children to be together just as you expect all of us, your children, to be together and to do things together."

"In what ways do we worship God?" their father continued.

"In many ways," his son answered.

In response to his statement, "Name some of them," the children mentioned, "Going to Church, singing hymns and songs, praying, giving our offering, reading and studying and memorizing the Bible, helping the poor and needy, singing in the choir, keeping the Church clean, cutting the grass, sweeping out the dirt, being honest with our money, and getting good grades in school."

Rev. Mr. Bode, rector of Castle Camps, Cambridgeshire, England, nodded approvingly at the answers his children gave. Then he said, "There is one more thing we ought not to forget in our definition of the Church. The people who make up the Church gather together to worship God. But people have many different ideas of God. Some think He is an angry deity, hurling sickness, disease and death to people who disobey Him. Others regard Him as a stern and heartless judge, sentencing His enemies to eternal torment just for the fun of seeing them suffer. Some religious people consider God their own private property and will not admit that anyone else except those who believe exactly as they do about God can love Him and serve Him. In what way is the Christian Church different?"

"Jesus makes the difference," the second daughter replied, "so the Church is a group of people who gather together to worship God as Jesus taught us."

"Correct," her father stated emphatically. "Jesus does make the difference. We worship a God of love, a heavenly father, who loves us like Jesus loved his disciples, and as the prodigal's father loved his wayward boy. Without Jesus, we would not know this kind of a God. Now, to get on with our review, what is a sacrament?"

The boy replied, "Something sacred and holy, and we have two sacraments in the Church, Baptism and the Lord's supper."

"How many modes of baptism are there?"

"Three: immersion, pouring and sprinkling."

"Is one method any more or less Christian than any other?"

"No," his son said. "It is not the amount of water or the way it is administered but the condition of the believer's heart that determines whether he is accepted of God or not."

"What about the Lord's Supper?" his father continued.

"In the Lord's Supper we use the symbols of bread and wine. The bread represents Jesus' body broken for us, and the wine His blood of the new covenant, shed for many for the remission of sins."

"How do we serve God," the pastor asked again.

"We serve Him by remembering the words of the one-hundredth Psalm," his daughter replied. " 'Serve the Lord with gladness.' That means that we are serve Him gladly and at the same time serve Him by being glad ourselves all the time. 'Come before His presence with singing' means that we serve God by singing hymns and songs of praise. 'Enter into His gates with thanksgiving and into His courts with praise.' We go to His house with grateful hearts for the gift of the Church and to worship Him for His goodness with praises upon our lips. 'Give thanks unto Him and bless His name.' In our prayers we express our thanks for His blessings and reverence His name."

"Excellent!" the proud father exclaimed. "Now, in closing, give me some of the terms by which Jesus was known and by which we know Him today."

The other girl spoke up immediately. "Jesus is called the Son of God as well as the Son of Man. Some called Him Rabbi, Teacher, Master and Friend, while others knew Him as Saviour, Redeemer, Messiah and Lord. Jesus is His earthly name, His human name; Christ is His heavenly name, His title as God's Anointed."

Her father nodded in approval. Then, going to his desk, he picked up a sheet of paper and said to his children, "For some time now I have been thinking of your coming confirmation, of the time when my children would take their places as members of the Church of our Lord and Saviour, Jesus Christ. I wanted to be sure that you would understand what all of it meant, and knew what you were doing, according to your age and relative intelligence. You have gladdened my heart by the way you have learned what I have tried to teach you. In order to crystallize these thoughts in your minds, I have written a hymn containing all of the important truths I want you to remember when you are finally confirmed. I have prepared this hymn in six stanzas of eight lines each. Some day you may wish to sing it. In that event, you will want to pick out a suitable and appropriate tune. Meanwhile, let me read the words for all of you to hear." With that, he began to read his original confirmation hymn which he had but recently prepared:

O Jesus, I have promised To serve Thee to the end;
Be Thou forever near me, My Master and my Friend;
I shall not fear the battle If Thou art by my side,
Nor wander from the pathway, If Thou wilt be my Guide.

Eight years after this experience, the poet-preacher died at Cambridgeshire, October, 1874. Although he wrote several volumes of verse and was honored by being invited to deliver the Bampton Lectures at Oxford, he is remembered today for this beautiful hymn, and takes his rightful place in the ranks of the "one hymn" poets, whose single poems make up the greater part of today's hymnody. That it is worthy of a permanent place cannot be denied, for a clearer expression of Christian devotion, and a more sincere and earnest prayer to that end, would be impossible to find, for children, as well as for young people and adults.

O PERFECT LOVE, ALL HUMAN THOUGHT TRANSCENDING

"All through with the invitations?" Dorothy Bloomfield asked her younger sister.

"All through," the other girl replied, "and what a job it was. I thought we would never get them addressed, much less signed, sealed, stamped and mailed. I didn't know getting married was such a task. I feel like I've been in a mad whirl for the past three weeks, and I'm almost beginning to wonder if marriage is worth it," she sighed, as she threw herself on the sofa for a few moments of needed relaxation.

"It's worth it, all right," Dorothy replied. "Many girls would gladly go through three months or even three years of such whirling to get a husband like Hugh."

"I'm fortunate, Dorothy, and I know it. Just think, in less than a week I will be Mrs. Hugh Redmayne. I'll have to get used to that name, you know."

"You'll get used to it all right," her older sister said. "Just be sure the wedding goes off as planned, and without a hitch. Check your list, will you? I just want to be sure we have done everything we are supposed to do."

The weary bride-to-be got up from the sofa, walked over to the desk and picked up a piece of paper. With a heavy sigh she began to read: "Invitations—recording gifts as they arrive—acknowledge all gifts after the honeymoon." She paused and glanced over at her sister. "Well, that won't have to be done until we come back." Then, resuming her reading, she continued: "Flowers—wedding dress—gifts for the attendants—check with the caterer—plenty of punch and cake at the reception—luggage—tickets—thanks for those who gave me showers—I think some girls get married just to get away from the ceaseless round of showers and parties."

"And some girls elope for the very same reason," her sister added.

While Dorothy began straightening up the living room, gathering up the boxes in which gifts had been packed, and giving the house a semblance of order, her younger sister went over to the piano and began to relieve her weariness with music. She played through several familiar selections and then began thumbing through the hymnal. From the next room, Dorothy soon heard her singing the first stanza of "O strength and stay, upholding all creation," a translation of an ancient Latin hymn by Ellerton and Hort, which had been published for the first time just twelve years earlier, in the 1871 edition of "Church Hymns." Finishing her chores, Dorothy joined her sister at the piano and they both sang the second stanza of the poem, reputed to have been a work of St. Ambrose, to the tune 'Strength and Stay,' by Rev. John B. Dykes:

Grant to life's day a calm, unclouded ending, An eve untouched
    by shadows of decay;
The brightness of a holy deathbed blending, With dawning
    glories of eternal day.

"That is still my favorite hymn, Dorothy," the young girl said. "The mood of the music seems to match that of the stanzas unusually well. I hope our wedding day will be marked by a 'calm unclouded ending.' "

"I'm sure it will, dear," Dorothy added. "I just want to feel that we have done everything humanly possible to make it all that a girl's wedding day ought to be. It comes only once in your lifetime and it should be as perfect as possible," she continued.

Rising from the piano bench, the young sister embraced Dorothy tenderly. "I am so grateful for everything you are doing to make my dreams come true, Dorothy," she said. "I hope to be able to do as much for you when you are married."

"I'm sure you will, dear," Dorothy said lovingly. "I'll keep you posted if and when the day ever arrives. Now, is everything else in order?"

"Oh," her sister said in reply. "The wedding music. I forgot to list the music for the organist and the soloist."

During the next half-hour the two girls selected the music for the wedding and made several copies of their choices for those who would be participating in the ceremonies. When they were through, the young girl looked up at her sister and said, "Dorothy, why not write a new hymn for my wedding."

"Who?" Dorothy asked.

"Why you, darling," her sister replied. "You are a poet, you know, and what is the use of having a sister who can write poetry if she cannot prepare a new hymn for her sister's wedding."

"To what tune?" Dorothy asked, trying to wiggle out of her new assignment.

"To 'Strength and Stay,' my favorite hymn tune," her sister answered.

Dorothy repeated the lines of the first stanza, counting the syllables on her fingers. "The first and third lines have eleven syllables and the second and fourth have ten," she explained.

"That's right," her sister added. "Now why don't you write another hymn in the same poetic meter so it can be sung to my favorite tune."

Dorothy, resigned to her fate, rose, picked up a hymnal, and said, "If no one will disturb me, I'll go into the library and see what I can do."

"I'll stand guard at the door and see that no one bothers you until you are finished," her sister said, walking with her to the adjoining room.

Once inside the library of their home, Pull Wyke, Windermere, England, twenty-five-year-old Dorothy sat in one of the easy chairs and pictured the wedding that was about to take place. When, in her mind's eye, she saw the bride and groom kneeling in prayer before the altar of the Church, the words fairly leaped into her heart, and she wrote down as rapidly as possible these lines:

> O perfect love, all human thought transcending,
> Lowly we kneel in prayer before Thy throne;
> That theirs may be the love which knows no ending,
> Whom Thou forevermore dost join in one.

Her stanzas carried out the theme of the perfect union of love and life as they are found in God's revelation in Jesus. To her sister's delight, the stanzas were as perfect as the theme about which they had been built, and the new hymn was sung at the wedding a few days later, in the summer of 1883.

Dorothy later became Mrs. Gerald Gurney, and it is under her married name that the famous wedding hymn now appears. Later Barnby's tune supplanted that of Dykes, and, following its use at the wedding of the Duke of Fife and Princess Louise of Wales on July 27, 1889, it enjoyed widespread popularity, being used in similar ceremonies throughout the Christian world.

Although the poet produced several volumes of poems and devotions before her death in 1932 at the age of seventy-four, she is remembered today for the wedding hymn she wrote at her young sister's request half a century before her passing. Her blending of perfect love and life is still an ideal for couples though all ages who seek to honor God through their marital union.

O SACRED HEAD NOW WOUNDED

"Do not sign," Rev. Paul Gerhardt cried out from his sick bed to his brethren of the ministry. "Do not sign. If we are Lutherans, let us prove our loyalty to our faith. We have yielded on point after point to Frederick Wilhelm, and now this has come upon us as a result of our previous compromises. You cannot meddle with tyrants. They will break you to their will when it suits their pleasure, and at their convenience."

As his comrades of the ministry gathered about the sick bed of their distinguished pastor and co-worker, minister of the great St. Nicholas' Church, Berlin, Germany, their spokesman in the current conflict, Gerhardt pleaded with them more earnestly than before, "As Christian ministers we cannot agree to the signing of any document that will silence our tongues and seal our lips. It is one thing to admit the Reformed point of view in a theological debate, but it is quite another thing to be told that we cannot call their views in question in our public religious services. If the Great Elector of Brandenberg thinks he can silence us in this way, he is sorely mistaken."

"But, Paul," a brother pastor counselled, that afternoon in 1665, "you have suffered enough already. None of us has gone through what you have gone through or been called to endure what you have had to endure. This may mean that you will be deprived of your pulpit and your livelihood. Frederick Wilhelm may actually depose you if you refuse to comply with his request."

"Request? Did you say 'request'?" the fifty-eight-year-old pastor replied. "It is an order, a command, not a request. And if it means being deprived of my pulpit, I still have my life."

True, he had had more than his share of suffering, and his brother ministers knew it only too well. The Peace of Westphalia had ended the bloody Thirty Years War in 1648 and Gerhardt had only then continued his preparation for the Christian ministry. Consequently, with almost half of his life behind him, he had reached his forty-fourth birthday by the time he was ordained to the ministry and appointed to his first parish, Mittenwald, in 1651. During his six years there, he married the great love of his life, a former pupil, Anna Marie Barthold, in 1655, being forty-eight years of age at the time. In the intervening ten years between their marriage and his exhoration to the ministers to defy their ruler, of the five children that had blessed their union, four had died in infancy. A son, Paul Frederich, alone was left to comfort the hearts of his parents in their nights of tragedy and sorrow. The pastor, however, had refused to give way to despair and melancholia. The one sustaining factor in his life had been the knowledge of God's providential care and boundless love, and his confidence that God had neither forgotten nor forsaken him. Turning from some of the harsher doctrines of Luther's theology, he had found solace and strength in his experience of this love and care.

Already he had put some of his feelings into poetic form, and as recently as 1653 had written a poem, which, translated by John Wesley into English in 1736 became the hymn, "Jesus, thy boundless love to me, No thought can reach, no tongue declare; O knit my thankful heart to thee, And reign without a rival there!" Again, three years later, he had composed another which Wesley translated in 1739, giving us the hymn so descriptive of the lives of both author and translator, "Give to the winds thy fears." From that same era, he wrote a Christmas carol which Catherine Winkworth rendered from German into English in 1858, "All my heart this night rejoices, While I hear, Far and near, Sweetest angel voices." If the loss of loved ones could not break him, neither could a command from the Elector. So he refused to sign the edict and was immediately deposed from his pulpit in retaliation. However, the people of Berlin had learned to love and appreciate the fearless clergyman and they just as quickly rallied to his support. The Elector was besieged with petitions and delegations urging him to reinstate the popular pastor. Even the Town Council as well as the Elector's own wife interceded in his behalf. The result was that the minister was given back his pulpit, at the same time that the ruler sent him this brief message, "I know that you will now, without constraint, agree to do that which I have been compelled to extort from the other Lutheran clergymen."

Gerhardt was unyielding. "I fear," he said, "that if I should accept my office under these conditions, I should draw on myself God's wrath and punishment."

Worn by the conflict, his dear wife, after just thirteen years of marriage, died in 1668. Left a widower with one son, Gerhardt was transferred to Lubben, in Saxony, where he spent his remaining days "in sadness, loneliness and affliction." But out of his heart flowed hymn after hymn, until he had written one-hundred-thirty-two masterpieces, in over fifty different metrical patterns. These hymns reflect his own personal experiences as he practiced his faith in his own life, his home, his parish, his church and his world. Being more intimate and personal than most of the hymns of Martin Luther, they were quickly accepted by the Christian community and widely used by the German people.

While "Jesus thy boundless love to me," "Give to the winds thy fears" and "All my heart this night rejoices" are direct translations from the original German, his noblest hymn is actually a translation of a translation. The year after he moved to Berlin, and was already gaining fame as a hymn writer, Gerhardt discovered a Latin poem which was ascribed to the twelfth century saint, Bernard of Clairvaux. He was so impressed with its beauty that he translated it from Latin into German, the hymn being known by its first line, "O Haupt voll Blut und Wunden." Almost three centuries later, a Virginia-born Presbyterian minister, James Waddell Alexander, caught the spirit of the German, which had been a decided improvement upon the original Latin, and translated Gerhardt's poem into the English masterpiece, "O sacred head now wounded with grief and shame weighed down." The first translator's own life is reflected in the closing lines of this superb passion hymn, for in them he prays, "O make me thine forever And should I fainting be, Lord, let me never, never, Outlive my love to thee."

Coupled with a tune by Hans Leo Hasler, composed in 1601 for a German love song, but harmonized into greatness by

Johann Sebastian Bach in 1729, this is as majestic and as profound a hymn as Christendom has ever produced. Out of their personal tragedies, the author and composer gave the world a hymn of sorrow that is permeated with the spirit of triumph, a passion hymn that is in reality a paean of praise.

O ZION HASTE, THY MISSION
HIGH FULFILLING

"Why don't other children know about Jesus, mother?" little Betty Thomson asked her mother, thirty-four-year-old Mrs. Mary Ann Thomson, from her sick bed one afternoon in 1868.

"Because no one has gone to tell them the good news of Jesus and His love," her mother replied.

"Then to whom do they pray when they are sick?" the little girl asked.

"If they don't know about God and Jesus, they have no one to pray to," her mother explained.

"And no Bible to read from?" the child continued.

"No, dear. If they don't know about Jesus, they don't have a Bible," she answered.

The girl was silent for a few moments, and then said, "It must be awful to be sick and not have a God to pray to and Bible stories to read. It's just like the song we learned in Sunday School, mother."

"Which one was that?"

" 'I think when I read that sweet story of old,' " the child began, "and the chorus went like this:

But thousands and thousands who wander and fall
Never heard of that heavenly home;
I wish they could know there was room for them all,
And that Jesus has bid them to come."

"That's true, Betty," her mother said. "There are thousands of children here in America as well as in other parts of the world who have never heard about Jesus and His love, and the room in His heart as well as in His heavenly home for each one of them."

"When I grow up, mother, I think I'll be a missionary," the

child said, "and tell some of these children what it means to love Jesus and be a Christian."

"Your father and I will be so happy if you decide to do that, Betty," her mother said. "You could do nothing nobler with your life than to publish the glad tidings of Jesus, the tidings of redemption and release. You see, dear, the fathers and mothers need to know the story just as much as the children do."

"And I'll tell them that when they are sick, Jesus will send His angels to stand by their beds until they get well again," Betty continued, "and I'll tell them that Jesus is the light of the world so they won't be afraid of the dark."

To comfort her little daughter, Mrs. Thomson, London-born wife of John Thomson, librarian of the Free Library of Philadelphia, Pennsylvania, and a member of the Church of the Annunciation in that city, went to the piano in the next room and played through several beautiful hymn tunes. When she came to "Hark, hark my soul, angelic songs are swelling," she sang a couple of stanzas to the tune "Pilgrims" by Henry Smart. "This is my favorite tune," she said to Betty, as the child listened intently from the adjoining room.

"I like it, mother," Betty called out. "Sing some more verses."

Her mother played and sang until her daughter had fallen fast asleep. Then, moved by their conversation about the need for people to spread the good news of Jesus and His love, and with the strains of her favorite hymn tune ringing in her ears, Mrs. Thomson picked up some paper and a pencil, tip-toed into her daughter's bedroom, sat in a comfortable chair near the foot of the bed, and began to write a hymn. The first stanza began:

O Zion, haste, thy mission high fulfilling, To tell to all the
    world that God is light;
That he who made all nations is not willing, One soul should
    perish, lost in shades of night.
Publish glad tidings, tidings of peace; Tidings of Jesus, redemp-
    tion and release.

In half an hour, as Betty lay nearby sound asleep, she completed the six stanzas of her new hymn. Later she said to her husband,

"I wrote my lines to be sung to Henry Smart's tune for 'Hark, hark my soul.' " Sitting at the piano, she sang her stanzas to the tune with which he was familiar.

"It will make a fine missionary hymn, Mary," he told her, "and if Betty is never able to go herself, the hymn she inspired may move others to spread the glad tidings."

Eight years after this scene had taken place in Philadelphia, and unknown to the participants there, two musicians met in the home of James Walch, Bolton, Lancashire, England. Forty-year-old Walch, organist, choir director and composer, explained to his friend that afternoon in 1876, "I invited you over to hear a new hymn tune."

"To what hymn?" his friend asked.

"Faber's 'Hark, hark my soul,' " Walch answered.

"Good heavens, man," his friend said. "Isn't that hymn burdened down with enough tunes now?"

"Maybe so, but none of them suit my fancy," the older composer replied. "Take Dykes' tune, 'Angel's Song.' It is all right for a choir to sing as an anthem, but for congregational singing, it has too many high F's to make it practical. I'm afraid the people's voices would crack before they finished the second stanza."

"What about Henry Smart's tune 'Pilgrims'? It certainly is popular here in Lancashire."

"I know that only too well," Walch explained, "but it falls short of my idea of a perfect hymn tune."

"Then let me hear yours," his friend added, "and judge it for myself."

Walch sat down at the keyboard and played through his tune, after which his friend commented, "That is too good a tune to be printed as an alternate for 'Hark, hark my soul.' Don't you know of a stirring poem that needs just the kind of music you have composed?"

"No, I don't," the older man replied. "The metrical pattern, 11.10.11.10, with refrain, is a bit unusual, you know, and it won't be easy to find another good poem to fit it. However, if a first class hymn would fall into my lap, like manna from heaven, that would be a different matter."

It didn't fall into Walch's lap, but an editor of a new hymnal took Walch's new tune for "Hark, hark my soul," composed in England in 1876, and matched it with Mrs. Thomson's poem, written in America in 1868, to fit Smart's tune "Pilgrims," and came up with as perfect a blending of words and music as one could desire. Walch's music was henceforth known by the name "Tidings," and "O Zion, haste" is regarded universally as one of the most stirring hymns of the nineteenth century. While Walch lived until 1901 and Mary Ann Thomson until 1923, neither ever achieved the heights they reached in the hymn on which they unknowingly collaborated, although they never met each other, and little dreamed such a union of words and music possible. By means of their exhortation for "sons to bear the message glorious" and daughters to "publish the glad tidings," other people's sons and daughters have heeded the missionary call and spread to the four corners of the globe the "tidings of Jesus, redemption and release."

ONE SWEETLY SOLEMN THOUGHT

"I think we'd better go back to Ohio," Alice Cary said, as she caught her breath at the top of the third flight of steps. "Pulling these stairs day after day is about to get me down. We should never have left home in the first place," she added, as she unlocked the door to the little back third-story bedroom which she and her sister called home.

"We're here in New York City and we're going to stay here until we establish ourselves," her twenty-eight-year-old sister, Phoebe, replied. "We came here together and we're going to stay here together, and if there's any going home planned, we'll go home together," she added, firmly. "We'll rise or fall as the Cary sisters. After all, don't forget that it was the success of your volume of 'Poems' that made us decide to come here in the first place."

"But I didn't know that New York City would be such a hard nut to crack," Alice, four years Phoebe's senior, explained. "It's one thing to be a literary success in rural Ohio and quite another to make a name for yourself as a writer and a poet in a big metropolis. At least I've learned that much in the last two years," she continued. "And if the next two years are going to be as tough as the last two, it's 'Goodbye, Broadway' as far as I'm concerned."

The story of the two devoted Cary sisters had captured the imagination of the literary world, when, encouraged by the success of Alice's first book, published in 1850, they decided to leave rural Ohio and invade the crowded streets and the teeming cross-roads of the nation's largest city. Their mutual affection attracted the sympathetic interest of many other unknown writers and would-be poets, who followed their careers with unusual concern and admiration. But Alice was right. Two years later they were still right where they started.

"If it hadn't been for Mary, we would be in a bad way, sure

134

enough," she added. "I almost feel like the prodigal son in the pig pen, remembering that in father's house there is room enough and to spare."

"What do you want to do about it?" Phoebe asked. "Go back and say to Dad, 'We made a mistake when we left home. We have failed. Now make us two of your hired servants.'"

"You know I don't mean that, Phoebe," Alice replied. "Mary has been good to us to let us stay here month after month, owing rent as we do. It's just that I'm sensitive about living off the good graces of other people when we ought to be paying our own way, and sending some money back home instead of being on the borrowing end all the time. And this little third-story room isn't exactly my idea of home," she continued.

Phoebe smiled, "Nor mine, either," she added. "But, like John Howard Payne said, 'Be it ever so humble, there's no place like home.' Don't forget, Alice, that the man who wrote those lines never had a home to call his own. He wrote them in Paris and when he died, he was buried in Tunis, North Africa, thousands of miles from the home he immortalized in his famous poem. If he could write his name into immortality under those circumstances, why can't we?"

The following Sunday morning, in the early fall of 1852, Alice and Phoebe Cary attended services in a nearby Church, and were much impressed by the sermon delivered by their minister, Rev. George B. Cheever. As they walked back to the house owned by their friend and landlady, Mrs. Mary Clemmer Ames, they discussed the sermon. "His idea of heaven was different, didn't you think so, Phoebe?" Alice asked.

"Yes, Alice," Phoebe replied. "He said that Jesus' words about 'many mansions' didn't refer actually to large spacious mansions as we picture them, but to stopping-off places on a long journey, where one rested up and was refreshed and then began another stage of the journey to the next stopping-off place."

"That seems to be more like my conception of heaven," Alice commented. "While it may sound thrilling, life in a large mansion could be a nightmare to one who is accustomed to the crowded and cramped quarters of our little room. And his idea of heaven as a continuous journey into newer areas of life and larger spheres of influence appealed to me very much."

As they walked slowly up the three flights of stairs to their room, Phoebe said, "The finest thing he said, though, came at the close of his message. I think I can quote him word for word. 'We should never think of heaven as a store or a theatre, nor as a park or a business house, or even as an office building or a bank, or as a White House or a Capitol, but always as a home. So we are to live here as a family so that we may be ready for life in God's great family hereafter.'"

A few minutes later, Mrs. Ames knocked at the door and invited the sisters to be her guests for Sunday dinner, an invitation they accepted quickly and enthusiastically. That evening, still intrigued by the sermon of the morning, Phoebe read through the book of Revelation, noting the passages that referred to immortality and life after death. After a while she looked up at her sister and said, "Alice, every day we work together here, we are nearer making the dream of owning our own earthly home a reality, aren't we?"

"Yes, Phoebe; we are," she replied.

"And isn't it also true that every day we live for God here, we are nearer our heavenly home?" Phoebe asked.

"Yes," Alice answered, thoughtfully.

"Then why can't I write a hymn about it in this vein," Phoebe continued:

"One sweetly, solemn thought, Comes to me o'er and o'er— I am nearer home today Than I ever have been before."

"Why not?" Alice replied. "Go ahead with it and see how it comes out."

Phoebe Cary concentrated on her new poem for over an hour. When she read Alice the nine four-line stanzas, her older sister was pleased with the result and congratulated her on having written so beautifully on a theme neither had developed before.

Deserved success finally came to the two talented sisters, and they were able to move into their own home on Twentieth Street, New York City, not many months after Phoebe had penned her finest poem. In cooperation with the pastor of the Church of the Strangers, Dr. Deems, they prepared a volume of hymns which was published in 1869 and used there for many years. In all, Phoebe and Alice produced four volumes of hymns and religious poems. Her older sister's death in 1871, after a long and trying illness, came as such a crushing blow to Phoebe, that she survived her but five months, passing away in Newport, Rhode Island, on July 31 of that same year, at the age of forty-seven. She died in the spirit of her own stanzas which contained these beautiful lines about a Christian's death:

Father, perfect my trust; Let my spirit feel in death
That her feet are firmly set On the rock of a living faith.
Feel as I would when my feet Are slipping over the brink;
For it may be, I'm nearer home—Nearer now, than I think.

ONWARD CHRISTIAN SOLDIERS

The only musician ever to be mistaken for a world champion prize fighter was England's famous Arthur S. Sullivan. And then it was his name and not his physique that caused the mix-up. Sir Arthur was on an extended tour of the United States following the successes of his light operas in England and in many eastern seaboard cities of North America, when he and his travelling companion found themselves in a California mining camp. The distinguished composer was being introduced to some of the miners, when a huge giant of a man with a coal-begrimed face and an iron grip stepped forward and took the Englishman by the hand.

"Mr. Sullivan," he said, with deep emotion, "it is an honor for me to meet you, sir. Just think, here I am shaking hands with John L. Sullivan, the heavyweight boxing champion of the world."

Sir Arthur burst into laughter as his companion hastened to explain to the boxing enthusiast, "He isn't John L. Sullivan, but Sir Arthur Sullivan, a famous composer from England."

"Oh," said the disappointed miner. "I'm sorry you're not John L. but still I'm glad to meet you anyway."

Whether the great John L. was ever mistaken for Sir Arthur has not been determined, but doubtless had the pugilist been introduced to a cultured circle of English society that same year, an equally confusing situation could well have resulted.

Unfortunately, Sir Arthur was not blessed with the iron constitution which his American "namesake" enjoyed. He was plagued with ill health for years, composing and orchestrating some of his most delightful music when he was suffering most intensely from persistent illness. That he could overcome physical pain to the extent that he did is a tribute to his sterling character as well as to his spirit of determination.

He was not the first person to house a lilting soul in a pain-wracked body. Madame Guyon, who wrote many of her nine hundred hymns while imprisoned in France's horrible Bastille for exercising her religious faith according to the dictates of her conscience, lost her radiant physical beauty through the ravages of smallpox when she was twenty-four. Yet the inner beauty of her soul illumines every line of her writings. And Rev. Timothy Dwight, president of Yale for many years, penned "I love thy kingdom, Lord" and other well-known hymns despite the fact that he was half-blind and pock-marked by the same dread disease. He was a great sufferer all his life as a result of having been deliberately inoculated with smallpox after the fashion of his day.

Sullivan was already heralded as a successful composer at twenty-nine, when he was invited to spend a few days at "Hanford," the home of Mrs. Gertrude Clay-Ker-Seymer, in Dorsetshire, England, early in 1871. While staying there, he came across the stanzas of "Onward Christian Soldiers" which Rev. Sabine Baring-Gould had written six years earlier, in 1865, for the children of his parish at Horbury Bridge to sing during a Whit Monday march to an adjoining parish for a holiday outing. He recalled that the hymn had been originally sung to Baring-Gould's arrangement of a theme from Haydn's Symphony in D. But, as he studied the words, he felt inspired to try his own hand at composing a tune that would match the vigor, movement and enthusiasm of the words. (That he was eminently successful is proven by the universal acclaim and widespread usage which greeted his music.) Composing in the florid style of his day, he soon completed the new tune, naming it for his hostess, "St. Gertrude."

Later that evening he introduced it to the assembled members and guests of the household in the private Chapel that was attached to the house. It was printed in a journal that same year, and included in a hymnal the following year, 1872. That year he also composed the tune "Hanford," named for the place where he had written his finest tune. Originally prepared for Charlotte Elliott's poem, "Jesus, my Saviour, look on me," it is now sung to another of her devotional poems, "My God, my Father, while I stray."

Almost thirty years after this incident, Mrs. Clay-Ker-Sey-

139

mer recalled with understandable pride the part she played in the creation of a tune which now enjoys such world-wide fame.

Sullivan's twenty-six hymn tunes which were included in "Church Hymns" which he edited in 1874 showed a decided improvement over his first hymn tune "The Homeland," which is dated 1867. Once he set his genius to mastering a new field, he proved himself without a peer.

Queen Victoria honored him on three occasions: First, when she ordered a private performance of one of the Gilbert and Sullivan light operas for herself and the Prince of Wales; Second, when she knighted him in 1883; and finally, when she requested him to compose a hymn tune in honor of her Diamond Jubilee, such a request from royalty being tantamount to a command. Rudyard Kipling wanted Sullivan to have the first chance at composing a tune for his famous "Recessional," but the musician failed to take advantage of the poet's offer.

By his voluminous composing in many varied fields, he lifted English musical life to a higher level, teaching his countrymen that their contributions could equal those of many European composers to which the English had too long paid humble obeisance.

Today their pride in their music is due in no little measure to the efforts and labors of Arthur Sullivan, who, in the fifty-eight years of his life, created music that will live in the hearts and souls of men and women for generations to come. Like John L., he can be numbered among the world champions!

OUR BLEST REDEEMER

"This is your engagement ring, darling," Harriet Auber's fiancé said, as he slipped the lovely diamond on the fourth finger of her left hand. "Soon I hope to have the privilege of placing a wedding band on this same finger," he quickly added. Harriet looked at the sparkling diamond for a long time and then said, "Every time I fondle this ring, I will think of you, my sweet; and every time I see it reflect the rays of the sun, I will think of the love we bear each for the other."

He kissed her tenderly there in a secluded corner of the garden at Hoddsden, Herts, England, that romantic afternoon and then held her tightly as they both shrank from saying the words of farewell that they both knew they would soon have to speak. "Why must you go, dear?" she asked him plaintively, as they both sat on a bench over by the rose arbor. "We have no quarrel with the French, you and I. Let them stay on their side of the channel and leave us on our side," she continued. "Why must there always be war and fighting to separate lovers and shatter dreams and bring only loneliness and heartache in their wake?"

"It isn't a war of my choosing," he explained. "But I've been summoned and I must obey. Had I my way, we would forget all about guns and slaughter and run away to a lover's rendezvous in some secluded spot where no one would ever find us, and enjoy our love for the rest of our days."

He took her hands in his and squeezed them ever so tightly. Then, lifting her left hand to his lips, he kissed her engagement ring. "Let this be a precious bond between us until I come home to claim you for my own and to make you my bride," he said softly. After another fond embrace, he turned and walked quickly down the garden path to the east gate, never looking back for fear that his resolution to join his regiment would melt at the sight of her tears or that his determination to be a good soldier would disappear in the magic spell of another kiss. And off to the Peninsula Wars he went, leaving Harriet behind with memories of what had been and dreams of what might be in the future.

That May afternoon in 1809, thirty-five-year-old Harriet Auber walked up and down the familiar garden path fighting to hold back the tears and trying to shake off a premonition of doom that haunted her the moment her sweetheart closed the east gate behind him. Later that night she tried to concentrate on the revision of some of the poems she was preparing for a proposed book, but on every page she saw only his face and with the rustling of the papers heard only his voice. She thought, "How strange! My great grandfather, Pierre Auber, fled from Normandy to England in 1765 when the revocation of the Edict of Nantes drove the Huguenots from French soil. Now my beloved has to leave the free soil of England to fight in the hedge-rows of Normandy and there, possibly, to die."

The next few days passed slowly as she longed for some word about where he was and when his unit was to be shipped, but the mails were delayed and the despondency grew within her heart until she found it difficult to eat or sleep or concentrate on anything else other than his welfare. "The flame that keeps me alive is dying," she said, "and unless I hear from him soon, it will be but a flicker and then only cold and barren ashes."

Being devout by nature, she turned to the Bible seeking solace and strength and suddenly discovered that God was speaking to her through stories she had long since forgotten and words that had for years held for her no special meaning. Then it was that she reread the story of Jesus and His promise of a Comforter for His heart-broken followers, and she realized that the promise was made as much to her in the nineteenth century as it had been to the disciples of the first, and could be claimed by her as it had been by them hundreds of years earlier. Gradually she gained an inner composure and calm that was in direct contrast to her former state of tension and dismay.

With this spiritual experience came a heightening of her poetic and creative talents, and she worked faithfully, revising some of her poems and hymns, until she had used up every bit of writing paper in the house. Early one morning, several days later, before she had been able to replenish her supplies and resume her work, she felt, in an unusual way, the comforting presence of the Holy Spirit. She was a bit distraught when she could not lay her hands on writing materials immediately, but she suddenly remembered that Robert Burns was said to have scratched the words of "Comin' Thro' the Rye" on a pane of glass at Mauchline some years before. With that, she slipped her engagement ring from her finger, held it to her lips as she breathed a silent prayer for her lover's safety, and then, with the diamond, proceeded to trace the lines of a new hymn on the panes of her bedroom window. Her stanzas began with these words:

"Our blest Redeemer, ere He breathed, His tender, last farewell, A guide, a Comforter bequeathed, With us to dwell."

After two more stanzas, she concluded with these words:

"Spirit of purity and grace, Our weakness pitying see; O make our hearts Thy dwelling place, And worthier Thee."

Her fiancé was killed in the Battle of Waterloo six years later, and Harriet lived in "solitary splendor" in Hoddsden for more than half a century. Her "Spirit of the Psalms" was published in London in 1829, and included "Our Blest Redeemer" as one of two hymns written for Whit-Sunday (Pentecost).

Years after her death in 1862 at the advanced age of eighty-nine, this bit of verse alone remains from her pen to remind us that the promises of God in Christ Jesus are available to all His children in all their circumstances for all time to be.

PASS IT ON

The steward knocked at the stateroom door, and the lad inside called out, "Who is it?"

"It's the steward, sir, and I have your bill. May I come in?"

"My bill? What for?" the lad asked.

The steward tried the door, and, finding it unlocked, opened it and entered the tiny cabin. "The bill for your meals," he said, when he was inside the small room.

"Meals?" young Mark Pearse asked. "Right now I'm too sick to think about food. Anyway, I don't have any money," he added.

"No money?" the steward asked in surprise. "What do you think we are running here? A free boarding house?"

The sick lad groaned at the thought of food, but sat up on the side of his berth in order to explain his strange predicament. "I'm on my way home from Holland," he began, trying to win the sympathy of the older man. "I've been visiting in Zeist. Yesterday I arrived in Bristol and bought my ticket for the rest of the trip home. It took all the money I had so I thought it included the meals as well as the trip."

"Well, you know better now, young fellow," the steward interrupted, "and the sooner you pay up the better."

"Let me explain," Mark said. "I saw some people going into the dining room and no one asked them for tickets so I went on in with them, and no one asked me for a ticket either. And I saw some other people getting up from the tables and walking out and they didn't bother to pay anybody any money so I just assumed that the meals were included in the price of the ticket I bought for the trip home."

"Well, they weren't," the other replied. "And in cases like this, the only thing we can do to protect our interests is to take the passenger's luggage and keep it until the debt is paid in full," he continued.

The young boy clutched his stomach. "The way I feel now, I wish I had never eaten a mouthful, and as far as I'm concerned, I don't want another bite to eat until I get off this boat."

"That's all right with us," the older man said, "but it won't take care of the bill you owe us for what you have already eaten." Then, taking out a notebook and a pencil he asked, "What is your name and address?"

The lad answered, "My name is Mark Guy Pearse."

The steward wrote the name down and the lad then supplied him with his address, but the other man held his pencil poised in his hand as if he were deep in thought and did not write anything else down.

"What did you say your name was?" he asked, in a rather serious tone of voice.

"Mark Guy Pearse," the boy replied.

"Are you sure?"

"Of course I'm sure. I ought to know my own name, shouldn't I? Why?"

Without replying, the steward took off his gilt-banded cap and held out his hand to the bewildered youth.

"What's that for?" the lad asked, puzzled at the strange turn of events.

The older man said, "Young man, I should like to shake your hand."

"Why?"

"Some years ago my father died in England, and my mother was distressed at the thought of trying to provide for the family. During the early months of her widowhood, a man proved a staunch friend and looked after us when no one else seemed to care. That man's name was Mark Guy Pearse."

"That's my father," the lad said, excitedly.

"I know. I recognized your name immediately. I never thought the chance would come for me to repay the kindnesses he showed us during those trying days. But it has come, and I am grateful for the opportunity. I am going to pay your bill in full out of my own pocket in appreciation for what your father did for us when we had nothing."

As soon as the young traveller arrived safely at home, he told his father the story of what had happened aboard ship. The older man smiled. "See how a bit of kindness lives, my son?" he said. "He has passed it on to you and remember, if you meet anybody who needs a friendly hand, you must pass it on to him."

The father related the interesting story to his son-in-law, Rev. Henry Burton, a Wesleyan Methodist minister, who couldn't get the words "Pass it on" out of his mind. They gripped him and refused to let him go, until on April 3, 1885, he felt an inner compulsion to sit down and write a poem based upon that brief and catchy phrase. His five stanzas, set to music by George C. Stebbins, have sung their way around the world. The first lines were these:

Have you had a kindness shown? Pass it on!
'Twas not given for thee alone—Pass it on!
Let it travel down the years, Let it wipe another's tears,
Till in heaven the deed appears, Pass it on!

The lad grew up to become a famous London minister, while the poet gained renown as a writer and Biblical expositor, completing forty-one years in the pastorate in the United States, where he secured his education, and in his native England, to which his family returned in 1865 after a nine-year stay in America. In addition to this bit of verse, he is remembered as the author of the hymn "Break, day of God, O break," written on Christmas Eve, 1900 and "There's a light upon the mountain," penned in 1910. For many years his "Hymn for the sea" was sung at Sunday services on many ocean liners.

A more appropriate illustration of "Cast your bread upon the waters for you will find it after many days" (Ecclesiastes 11:1) would be difficult to find. And this incident should encourage all Christians "not to be weary in well-doing," since God has promised them that "in due season they will reap, if they faint not."

PRAISE GOD FROM WHOM ALL BLESSINGS FLOW

"Don't be foolish, Ken. If you do that it may cost you your life," a clergyman warned Rev. Thomas Ken (1637-1711). "After all, Charles II is King, for good or ill."

Ken stood his ground firmly. "I will not permit even the King of England to house his mistress beneath my roof," he said. "If His Majesty has the ignorance to suggest it, I have the arrogance to refuse him. A woman of ill repute ought not to be endured in the house of a clergyman, least of all in that of the King's Chaplain."

"But, Ken . . ." his friend objected.

"Silence," Ken demanded. "Not for his kingdom will I comply with the King's commands."

To circumvent what he thought a most unreasonable request from Charles II, who asked Ken to let Nell Gwyn, the Monarch's mistress, be a guest in his home while visiting in Winchester, England, where a sumptuous new palace was being erected, the clergyman hired a builder to make some repairs in the house. The first thing the employee did was to take off the roof, which relieved Ken of any responsibility for the notorious Nell's entertainment.

But Charles II refused to reprimand or discipline the dynamic little clergyman. He stood in awe of him, although he did not confess that fact to the members of his dissolute court. On one occasion, Ken preached a very strong sermon in which he took the ruler to task for his open association with the Gwyn woman. "As John the Baptist warned Herod Antipas that he had violated the law of God by taking unto himself his brother's wife, so you, O King, are also guilty of violating God's law by taking unto yourself this woman as your mistress and openly flaunting your immorality before the British people," Ken thundered from his pulpit.

"But, Thomas," a fearful brother minister added, "don't forget what happened to John the Baptist. He lost his head!"

"And I will be willing to lose mine if it will bring Charles II to his senses," the fearless minister replied, without batting an eye.

The King knew in his heart that his Chaplain was right, so he hesitated to take any action against him. Once, on being asked were he was going as he left the court chamber, the King answered, "I must go hear Ken tell me my faults." His secret admiration was revealed when the Crown was about to appoint a successor to the late Bishop of Bath and Wells. Although many able men were suggested for the post, Charles II dismissed them all, saying, "Odd's fish! Who shall have Bath and Wells but little Ken who would not give poor Nelly a lodging!" So Rev. Thomas became Bishop Ken. His first act in his new exalted position was to forgo the customary and expensive consecration dinner. Instead, he gave the $500 the banquet would have cost to his favorite charity. Eight days later, the King suffered a stroke, and called for Ken, who persuaded the dying ruler to renounce his mistress and ask the Queen's forgiveness before he died. The King consented, and died "in the faith."

The same devotion to principle which won him his bishopric lost it for him a few years later. Having sworn fealty to the new monarch, James II, he felt that in good conscience he could not take an oath of loyalty to William and Mary as long as James, whom he felt had been unjustly deposed, was alive. He gave up his office in 1691, making his home with friends in Wiltshire until his death.

It was in 1709 that Ken gathered together some of his poetic works that had been many years in the making, and, after extensive revisions and corrections in some which had been printed as early as 1674 for his students in Winchester, had them published in their final corrected form. At the close of three splendid hymns, entitled "Morning Hymn," "Evening Hymn" and "Midnight Hymn" he included his famous four-line poem in long meter, now known familiarly as "The Doxology":

> Praise God from whom all blessings flow,
> Praise Him, all creatures here below;

Praise Him above, ye heavenly host;
Praise Father, Son and Holy Ghost.

Both the author and composer of this hymn spent some time in prison. Ken was kept in the Tower of London with six other Bishops who refused to read the King's "Declaration of Indulgence" from their pulpits. The composer, Louis Bourgeois (1510-1561) was imprisoned in Switzerland for harmonizing several melodies of hymns against the express commands of Geneva's ruler, theologian John Calvin, who demanded that all hymns be sung in unison or not at all. Later Calvin interceded for him, and he was released, devoting his composing talents from that day on to melodies instead of harmonies. From his pen came the famous musical setting of Psalm 100, known, to this day, as "Old Hundredth," which was first printed in the 1551 edition of "The Genevan Psalter," thus ante-dating Bishop Ken's words by almost a century and a half.

If Bourgeois and Ken had done no more than give the Church "The Doxology," believers the world over would rise up and call them blessed, because, in all hymnody, there is no loftier hymn of praise with which to open or close a service of worship, or to acknowledge God's gifts when presenting an offering, than the four lines which they bequeathed as their finest legacy.

SPIRIT OF GOD, DESCEND
UPON MY HEART

"Look, mother," the little boy called out. "What's the matter with that man over there?"

His mother looked in the direction in which her son was pointing, and saw an elderly man staggering down one of the main streets in Holborn, England, that November afternoon in 1860.

"Is he drunk?" the lad asked.

"I don't think so," his mother replied. "He does not look like that kind of man. I wonder what's the matter with him?"

Another passerby ran up to the older man, placed his arm about him and said, "Sir, is there anything I can do to help?"

The white-haired stranger nodded his head. "I think I'm going," he said softly. "Please get me a doctor." While the sick man clutched his heart, the other man helped him lie down right there on the sidewalk. As a crowd of the curious quickly collected, he called out, "Give the man room. He's dying. Give him room. And someone please call a doctor."

Two other men quickly pushed their way through the gathering. "I am a doctor," one of them said. "What's the trouble?"

"I was passing by when this older man grabbed his heart and began to stagger. I rushed up and put my arm about him to steady him a bit, and he told me he was dying."

At that moment, the aged man who had, a few minutes before, been calmly walking down the street on his usual afternoon stroll, heaved a sigh and breathed his last. The doctor confirmed his death after a brief examination. "He is dead," he announced, as the people slowly stepped back in surprise and a few men doffed their hats in respect. "Does anyone know his identity, or where he lived or who his people were?" Several came up for a close look, and one man said, "I know his face, but I can't recall his name."

The fourth person to step forward took one look at the body and said, "I know him, sir. He is the Reverend George Croly."

"Oh!" said the doctor. "I had met him on several occasions but I failed to recognize him. Someone call his family, please. Notify the family of the Rev. Mr. Croly so they can come and claim his body."

"How old was he?" the lad who had first noticed him, asked his mother.

"I don't know, dear," his mother answered.

A man who heard the boy's question turned and said, "He was eighty years old, son. He celebrated his eightieth birthday just last August."

Word soon spread through Holborn that one of its most distinguished elderly clergymen had died suddenly on a public street that afternoon. As the story went from house to house, street to street and church to church, many who had known, respected and loved the minister talked and reminisced about his life and work.

"I remember hearing him preach at St. Stephen's Church," one man told his next door neighbour. "Have you ever been there?"

"No," his friend remarked. "It's down in a poor part of London, isn't it?"

"Yes, it is."

"How did Croly ever happen to get that pulpit?"

"Well, when he heard that St. Stephen's had been closed for nearly a century, he took it as a challenge, re-opened the Church and preached so powerfully that soon people of all classes from all parts of London were crowding the pews at every service."

"Conservative man, wasn't he?" another asked.

"Yes, quite; in religion as well as politics."

But, those being the days when words and labels as "liberal," "fundamental," "latitudinarian" and "antidisestablishmentarian" were being bantered around freely, the simple, uncompromising and forthright preaching of George Croly had attracted attention and brought results.

"I read his novel 'Salathiel,' " one woman said to a close friend, "the one about the wandering Jew. It was a best seller, you know. In fact, it became quite a sensation, which shocked the parson no end. He used to say to us, 'To look at me you would not think me capable of writing a sensational· book, would you, now?' And we would laugh and say, 'That's right, parson. We wouldn't think it possible.' But what he lacked in a clergyman's income he made up for with his pen. And no one blamed him, because he had a wonderful way with words. I understand he wrote novels, biographies, satires and plays as well as historical and theological books," she continued, "to say nothing of his poems. He was always partial to them, and proud of them, too," she added.

Croly had had too much common sense to align himself with any of the warring factions pitted against each other in church as well as state. "Those fighters have strayed too far from the great simplicities of Jesus," he used to say. "The Lord Himself would hardly recognize them even though they claim to be defending the faith once delivered to the saints. I'm afraid He would find more saints in the slums than in that kind of society."

At the request of his congregation, he had prepared a hymnal, including psalms, hymns and spiritual songs, ten of the hymns coming from his own pen. This book, "Psalms and Hymns for Public Worship," saw only one printing, dated 1854, and the greater part of that edition was destroyed by fire. This did not dim the ardour of the pastor, though, and he kept on writing until the day he fell dead while taking his customary afternoon walk through the streets of Holborn. His one immortal hymn appeared in the book he prepared for his own people, and gives future generations an insight into the character and soul of the author, because a deeper and more profound prayer would be almost impossible to find. He began with this stanza:

Spirit of God, descend upon my heart; Wean it from earth, thru
    all its pulses move;
Stoop to my weakness, mighty as thou art, And make me love
    thee as I ought to love.

The writer to the Hebrews said "It is appointed unto men once to die" but he does not say were or when. Joseph Scriven, author of "What a friend we have in Jesus," drowned in a small creek a hundred yards from the Sackville home, Bewdley, Ontario, where he suffered his last illness. Adelaide Pollard, known for her poem, "Have thine own way, Lord," died suddenly in a New York City railroad station, while waiting for the Philadelphia train. And P. P. Bliss, author and composer of many gospel songs, including "Wonderful words of life" and "Let the lower lights be burning," died in a terrible train wreck near Ashtabula, Ohio. But George Croly was the only famous hymn writer to drop dead suddenly and dramatically on a busy city street. Fortunately that is not his one claim to fame. That consists in the stanzas of his surpassingly beautiful hymn, "Spirit of God, descend upon my heart."

SWEET HOUR OF PRAYER

"Mr. Mason, I've been offered a job as church organist," William Bradbury proudly told his friend, Dr. Lowell Mason, choirmaster at the Bowdoin Street Church, Boston.

"Wonderful, William," the older man said, enthusiastically. "I'm sure you can handle the position. Let me be the first to congratulate you."

Bradbury came by his love of church music naturally, since his father, a Revolutionary War veteran, had been an amateur choir director, and his mother a singer in several of her husband's choirs.

"Between what I learned from Sumner Hill and Calvin Allen," the young organist continued, "I ought to be able to hold down my new job all right. Mr. Hill taught me all the harmony I know, and Mr. Allen, a foreman of the Chickering Piano Company, has given me as thorough a knowledge of that instrument as a young man could want. Between the two of them, to say nothing of the experience I have had singing under your leadership, I'm not afraid to tackle it," he concluded. So, with the high hopes of youth, young Bradbury went to the new Church to meet with the Music Committee as well as to try out the new organ.

"Young man," the committee chairman informed him, "we are prepared to offer you $25 a year if you can qualify to fill the position of organist in our Church."

Never one to quibble over money when a big opportunity presented itself, the musician merely nodded his head politely and asked, "May I see the organ now?" The men adjourned to the sanctuary of the Church, the sexton unlocked the cover of the console, and Bradbury took his place on the organ bench. When the sexton had pumped up the bellows, he struck a chord on the great manual. To his dismay, the keys did not come back up into their regular position.

"What's this?" he asked the chairman. "Where's the boy to pull the keys back?"

"We haven't a boy, Mr. Bradbury," the chairman explained.

"But you said nothing about this in your letter," the organist protested. "And every church organist in Boston can tell you that, in older instruments of this type, the church always provides a young lad to pull the keys up when the organist pushes them down."

"Well," the chairman explained, "we were under the impression that our offer of $25 a year would include both the pushing down and the pulling up."

"But that is double work," Bradbury said, "and double work always calls for double pay. I'll push them down for $25 a year and pull them up for $25 a year, which means a salary of $50 a year," he continued.

With that, the committee men got their heads together in a quick huddle, after which their spokesman said, "Thank you very much for coming over, Mr. Bradbury. We are happy to have had the privilege of meeting you, and wish you well as you continue your musical career."

Since it did not take a Harvard graduate to figure that out, William Bradbury politely and rather coldly said his "Goodbyes" and left.

When his friend and mentor, Lowell Mason, twenty-four years his senior, heard what had happened to his young, talented friend, he immediately found an opening for him as a music teacher and instructor in Machias, Maine. Other jobs followed, until Bradbury was offered a position at the Baptist Tabernacle, in New York City. Together with Mason and Dr. Thomas Hastings, he promoted Children's Music Festivals and pioneered in composing songs, hymns and special selections for the rapidly expanding Sunday School movement in the United States. Later he and his brother became piano manufacturers, turning out the well-known Bradbury pianos for many years. Although he, in collaboration with Mason, Hastings, Root and others, published more than fifty books of hymns, songs, and miscellaneous sacred music, before his death at fifty-two, in 1868, he is remembered and loved today for having composed some of the finest tunes for hymns and gospel songs in the nineteenth century. His diversity of talent and his sense of musical adaptability can best be seen in his tune which made "Jesus loves me, this I know," the children's favorite the world over, and the moving spirit of the tune "Woodworth," composed in 1849, which made Charlotte Elliott's autobiographical poem, "Just as I am without one plea," the best loved invitation hymn ever written.

It was in 1853 that he composed the music for the passion hymn, " 'Tis midnight and on Olive's brow," while ten years later, he fashioned the dramatic rhythm of "On Christ the solid rock I stand." Just four years before his death, he finally sat at the keyboard and made a musical setting for a poem on the Twenty-third Psalm, entitled "He leadeth me, O blessed thought!" which he had cut out of a religious magazine, "Watchman and Reflector" three years earlier. The hymn tune "Aletta" as well as the music for "Even me" and "Asleep in Jesus" came from his fluent pen, taking their places alongside "There is no name so sweet on earth," "I think when I read that sweet story of old," and the older tune, with refrain, for "Take my life and let it be."

However, it was in 1859 that he gave the wings of song to two poems that have found a permanent place in Christian hymnody. The first tune bears his name, "Bradbury," and was composed for another children's hymn, "Saviour, like a shepherd lead us." As for the second, hardly a Sunday rolls around that it is not sung in thousands of Churches throughout the world, because, like James Montgomery's "Prayer is the soul's sincere desire," this hymn, "Sweet hour of prayer," expresses the universal longings and aspirations of believers the world over. Written by a blind English minister, William W. Walford, and dictated to a friend who took the poem with him to New York, where it was published for the first time in 1845, this hymn has an appeal that is due in large part to the simple melody created for it by William Batchelder Bradbury. While not as profound as blind Rev. George Matheson's "O love that wilt not let me go," it is more popular and more easily sung, because of Bradbury's tune "Sweet Hour."

While some of his publications enjoyed enormous success, one book, "Fresh Laurels," printed in 1867, selling more than a million copies, the young organist who insisted that he was worth as much money to pull up the organ keys as he was to push them down, must have rejoiced when he discovered that, while *that* Church may not have thought so, the Church universal thinks him worth his weight in gold. Because, with few exceptions, there are as many tunes by Bradbury in today's Hymnals and Song Books, as there are by any other composer.

TIS SO SWEET TO TRUST IN JESUS

"Isn't the day just perfect," Louisa M. Stead said to her husband.

"It's as lovely a day as I've ever seen," he replied. "The water off Long Island is as blue as blue can be. Let's pack a lunch and go down to the beach. Lily will enjoy the water and we can be back before four o'clock."

"It's all right with me," his wife said. "I'll make some sandwiches and fix some lemonade if you'll get Lily ready."

So, while the father gathered up some of the four-year-old girl's things, the mother prepared a picnic lunch, and within an hour the family was down on the beach off Long Island, New York, playing in the sand, splashing in the surf and enjoying a few hours of relaxation and rest.

"My cup runneth over," Mrs. Stead said to herself as she watched her husband and little girl playing on the beach that afternoon in the summer of 1890. Soon she was thinking over the chain of events that had brought her to that happy hour. A native of Dover, England, she had come to America in 1871 on a visit with her family. At a religious service in Urbana, Ohio, she had been so deeply moved by a speaker's call for Christian young people to volunteer for missionary service in China, that she had gone forward and given herself to that high and holy task. But, to her great sorrow, she had been rejected for active duty on account of her health. Although the door to China seemed to be slammed in her face, nevertheless, out of that disappointment, she wrote a song, which began, "Precious Jesus, Thou hast saved me, Thine and only Thine I am." While she herself could not go to China, her hymn was translated into that language and sung by Chinese Christians in many of the mission stations dotting that ancient land.

Later she had met Mr. Stead and they had married and God had blessed their union with a sweet little daughter. "What more could one ask of life," she often said, "than a devoted husband, and a precious baby and a feeling that one has finally found one's place in God's wonderful plan."

Coming out of her revery quite suddenly, she saw a little boy out in the water beyond the breakers, struggling against the wind and the undertow to get back to the shore. "Darling," she cried out to her husband, "that little boy seems to be in trouble."

Mr. Stead leaped to his feet and sized up the lad's desperate plight in a moment. Without hesitating, save to call to his wife to look after their daughter, he threw off his outer garments and plunged into the waves to rescue the drowning boy. Mrs. Stead saw him reach the lad's side, place a strong arm about him and begin the swim back to the shore. But the little boy kept struggling, pulling wildly this way and that, instead of yielding himself to the superior strength and skill of the older man. While his wife looked on in horror, she saw the two of them go down under the waves. In a moment they emerged, only to drop quickly out of sight again. She rushed over to where Lily was digging in the sand, picked the child up and held her tightly to her breast as cold chills trembled through her body. Rushing to the edge of the water, she called out over the turbulent waters, "Darling— Darling— Where are you? Where are you?" But the only answer was the echo of her own words thrown back at her by the wind and half-muffled by the waves.

Later that evening, the body of Mr. Stead was found by several life-guards who had been summoned to the scene of the tragedy. The next few weeks were dark and melancholy ones for the heart-broken mother and the bewildered little daughter. She sought solace in the Bible as well as in the hymns and songs of her faith.

"Anne Steele asked for a 'calm, a thankful heart, from every murmur free,' when her sweetheart was drowned the day before they were to be married," she told a friend a few weeks later. "And Joseph Scriven laid hold of the power of prayer when he suffered a similar experience that led to the writing of 'What a friend we have in Jesus,'" she continued. "And when I tried to sing 'More love to Thee, O Christ,' I remembered that Mrs. Prentiss had cried out for more love when she lost her two children in an epidemic some years ago. But I do not need to pray for love. God knows I love Him and I know He loves me. What I need is an extra measure of faith and trust to believe that His Providence is still at work, and that His hand can still guide me through the bleak, unknown future."

The following months were sad and lonely ones. Coupled with her grief was the added burden of providing for the support of her little family. One afternoon, when the pantry was empty and they had nothing left to eat, Mrs. Stead and Lily prayed that God would provide for them out of His bounties, since He was aware of their need and of their trust in Him. The next morning she found a large basket of provisions at the front door, and an envelope containing enough money to buy shoes for the little girl. "We trusted God," she told Lily, "and He has not failed us." Out of that experience, she was inspired to write a simple poem that began with these lines:

'Tis so sweet to trust in Jesus, Just to take Him at His word;
Just to rest upon His promise; Just to know "Thus saith the Lord."
Jesus, Jesus, how I trust Him; How I've proved Him o'er and o'er!
Jesus, Jesus, precious Jesus! O for grace to trust Him more.

Ten years after Mr. Stead lost his life, his widow married Rev. Robert Wodehouse. A native of South Africa, he met her while attending a missionary school in the United States. Following his ordination as a Methodist minister, Mr. and Mrs. Wodehouse were appointed by Bishop Hartzell to the Methodist mission at Umtali, Southern Rhodesia, where they labored faithfully for twelve years. Lily grew up to become Mrs. D. A. Carson, herself a missionary for many years in the same African station. She cared for her mother during the latter's final illness, until Mrs. Wodehouse passed away on January 18, 1917, at Penkridge, adjoining the Mutambara Mission. Her final resting place was chiselled out of solid rock on the side of Black Mountain near her African home. But the song she wrote out of her heartache has been a source of inspiration to millions of Christians the world over who have been inspired by her biographical lines to

face tragedy and sorrow in the spirit of the fourth stanza of her
finest hymn:

I'm so glad I learned to trust Thee, Precious Jesus, Saviour,
Friend;
And I know that Thou art with me, Wilt be with me to the end.

THE CHURCH'S ONE FOUNDATION

Rev. Samuel J. Stone never sought a fight, but he didn't back away from one, either, whether it was a physical or a theological one. He always said, "Had it not been for an irresistible call to the Christian ministry, I would have become a professional soldier." His friends usually added, "He would have made a first-class prize fighter, too. A man doesn't captain his college crew unless he has what it takes, and Samuel Stone had more than his share of steel muscles and iron determination."

When he graduated from Oxford, he went to serve his first appointment in the Church of England, the little mission in Windsor, across the river from Eton College and the Royal Castle. It was a tough neighbourhood but the minister was equal to every occasion. When he came upon a bully mistreating a small girl one day, he beat the community terror black and blue. The other "toughs" carefully avoided the rector from that day on, especially when the victim of the parson's righteous wrath reported that "he tore into me like an avenging angel." The minister later confessed that his anger had momentarily gotten the best of him, but those who knew the community were secretly glad that someone had had the fortitude to curb the gang of ruffians that had terrorized the area too long.

He became involved in a bitter dispute with civic authorities when public schools were opened in his parish. "They will conflict with our system of Church supported parochial schools," he protested vigorously, until a strong adherent of the other system denounced him as "the most tyrannical priest in East London."

He was a curious mixture of conservative and liberal ideas, fighting for the all-sufficiency of the Scriptures on one hand, and, on the other hand, opening his Church early in the morning so commuters could rest there between the time their trains arrived and their offices opened. The most famous as well as the most fruitful controversy in which he became involved broke in full fury in 1862, Stone's twenty-third year, when Rev. John Colenso, Bishop of the Anglican Church in Natal, South Africa, threw a theological bomb-shell into the ranks of Christendom with the publication of a book entitled "The Pentateuch and the Book of Joshua Critically Examined." When the distinguished clergyman got through "critically examining" the first five books of the Old Testament, he was ready to throw them out of the Holy Bible. Subjecting them to the analysis of the critics of the day, and basing his arguments entirely upon reason and science, his book was greeted with widespread furore on the part of those who believed in "the inerrant verbal inspiration of the Bible."

One of those who leaped into the fray was Samuel John Stone. "This kind of trash will destroy the Church," he argued, "and if it is allowed to go unchallenged will weaken our position for a thousand years." The challenge was met, however, by Colenso's superior, Bishop Gray, of Capetown, South Africa. He brought his subordinate to trial for heresy the very next year, 1863, the result being that Colenso was "condemned for his views, deposed from his position, and prohibited from the exercise of any divine office." The sentence was severe because his superiors considered his questioning of the inerrancy of the Bible a very severe crime.

When the "culprit" disregarded his sentence, he was excommunicated from the Church. The Crown reversed the judgement of the Church court, when the Privy Council declared the decision "null and void." But, for all intents and purposes, Colenso was finished in South Africa. Returning to England, he was supported by gifts from interested friends all over the island, and preached to large congregations whenever he had the opportunity. In many ways, he was far less pugnacious than his critics and demonstrated far more of the love of Christ than those who opposed him.

Stone rejoiced when Bishop Gray came to the defense of the Church and the Bible, and offered to participate in the series of debates that ensued. Out of this period of bitterness and wrangling, Stone, now twenty-seven, was inspired to write a series of poems based upon the phrases of The Apostles' Creed, in order to explain as well as strengthen and defend the official position of the Church. Cecil Humphreys had published her "Hymns for little children" in 1848, the year she married Rev. William Alexander, in which she included a series of hymns for children based on the statements in the historic Creed. But it had been many years since anyone had attempted the same thing for adults. And to that task, Samuel Stone set his heart and his hand.

When he came to the phrase "I believe . . . in the holy catholic Church," he rose to the occasion and penned his defense of the Church he loved and served in words that outlived their immediate setting and have endured after the situation that inspired them has been forgotten. He began with these superb lines:

The Church's one foundation Is Jesus Christ, her Lord;
She is His new creation, By water and the word.
From heav'n He came and sought her To be His holy bride;
With His own blood He bought her, And for her life He died.

The original seven stanzas were expanded to ten and then reduced to the four that are found in practically every hymnal in the English speaking world, because no grander hymn of the Church has ever been written. It was published as one of twelve creedal hymns in the author's "Lyra Fidelium" in 1866.

Now, wedded to the tune "Aurelia" (Golden), which was first matched with "Jerusalem The Golden," although it was composed originally for Keble's wedding hymn, "The voice that breathed o'er Eden," in 1864, its greatness and glory can best be summed up in one word, "magnificent."

Controversies come and controversies go, but this hymn reminds us again and again that "the Church is of God and will endure until the end of time."

THE SON OF GOD GOES FORTH TO WAR

The honor of being the first "native" American composer has been claimed by a friend of George Washington, Francis Hopkinson, (1737-1791). He himself wrote, "However small the reputation I shall derive from this work (His song "My days have been so wondrous free," composed in 1759), I cannot, I believe, be refused the credit of being the first native of the United States who has produced a musical composition.

But the honor of being known as "The Father of American Hymnology and Public School Music" is reserved for Lowell Mason (1792-1872), who began his work auspiciously in 1824, when, as organist and choir director of the Independent Presbyterian Church, Savannah, Georgia, he composed three of his finest tunes for the hymns, "Safely through another week," "When I survey the wondrous cross," and "From Greeland's icy mountains," the latter composed at the request of a young lady who was later to become the wife of one of the Church's pastors, Rev. Francis H. Goulding.

However, the honor of being known as the most prolific Christian poet in the history of the Americas has been bestowed upon Fanny Crosby (1820-1915), who, in her ninety-five years wrote more than eight thousand different poems on the widest variety of subjects imaginable. She is about the only famous poet who has written so voluminously that, on several occasions, she failed to recognize her own creations. When she heard Ira D. Sankey sing a lovely sacred song, "Hide me, O my Saviour, hide me," at the Northfield, Massachusetts Assembly Ground, she was so delighted with it she asked the nationally known song-leader, "Where did you find that song, Mr. Sankey?" He thought she was joking and passed off the request with a laugh and a gentle pat on the back. But when she put the same question to him later in the day, he realized that she was serious. "Where did I find it?" he said to her. "Why, you gave it to me yourself, Aunt Fanny. It is one of your own poems." Her amazement and embarrassment can well be imagined.

A few years later, the same thing happened again when she heard a lovely soprano singing "Valley of Eden, beyond the sea." When the woman sang the song a second time at Fanny Crosby's request, she suddenly recognized it as her very own. While she wrote more poems, Mason shares with Britain's John B. Dykes, the honor of having more tunes in standard hymnals than any other composer.

Another famous "first" involves the organist and choirmaster, Henry Stephen Cutler (1824-1902). In 1856 he was connected with the Church of the Advent in Boston. Although he knew of the scandal that had arisen over the presence of a choir of surpliced clergymen at a Choral Eucharist in New York City's Church of the Annunciation in 1852, he was daring enough to take a chance, and vested the boy's choir in his Church. He must not have shocked the worshippers as much as he expected to, because, in 1858, when he moved to Trinity Church, New York City, he decided to try the same thing on his new congregation. Fortunately, fate intervened at the providential moment, when His Royal Highness, the Prince of Wales, on a tour of the United States, notified the minister of his desire to attend a service at Trinity on October 11, 1860.

Since choirs in Anglican Churches were vested, it was deemed proper to vest the singers for this special gathering in the Prince's honor. Consequently, in order to have his choir members accustomed to appearing and singing in robes, he asked them to wear their new vestments for the first time on the Sunday morning preceding the Royal party's visit. So, on October 7, 1860, the singers appeared in their surplices, and wore them, apparently, without adverse criticism or comment. Whether Cutler's daring innovation cost him his job or not has not been definitely determined. Suffice it to say that while he was out of the city on a month's concert tour, the vestry dismissed him from his position in Trinity Church for being A.W.O.L., "Absent without leave." He terminated his services there on June 30, 1865, thus depriving Trinity from being the Church at whose organ console Cutler composed his one famous and lasting hymn tune. He subsequently held positions in Churches in

Brooklyn, Providence, Philadelphia and New York until his retirement in 1885.

Although Columbia University honored him with the Doctor of Music degree in 1864, it was not until 1872 that Cutler composed his splendid tune, "All Saints, New," for the hymn-poem Bishop Reginald Heber had written for St. Stephen's Day, over half a century before, "The son of God goes forth to war."

The fact that in most modern Churches the choir sings in robes and within the chancel is due in no small measure to the chances taken by Cutler in Boston and New York in the decade prior to the tragic Civil War. However, his precedents may have caused ecclesiastical wars and shattered age-old Church traditions, the results of which will be debated for generations to come.

THE SPACIOUS FIRMAMENT ON HIGH

"A writer does not have to be obscene to be brilliant," the editor of "The Spectator" announced. "The day will come when authors who openly and flagrantly violate the accepted standards of decency will not be honored as men of genius, but will be scorned and ridiculed as bearing the marks of a fool," he continued. And to prove his point, Joseph Addison (1672-1719) sat down at his desk in 1713 and wrote a brilliant play against a background of Imperial Rome, entitled "Cato." Little did this English man-of-letters dream, as he hammered out his lines, that his words would inspire two of the noblest patriotic utterances in the history of the United States of America. Nor did he apologize for "preaching and getting away with it" in his essays, news stories, poems and plays. After all, he was the son of an honored clergyman of the Church of England, and had himself seriously considered taking Holy Orders before plunging into the comparatively new fields of literature and politics.

Sixty-three years after "Cato" was first published, a twenty-one-year-old Captain in George Washington's Continental Army was sentenced by the British to be hung as a spy at 11 o'clock on the morning of September 22, 1776. As young Nathan Hale prepared to pay with his life for his devotion to his country, these lines from Act 4, Scene 4 of "Cato" flashed into his mind, "What pity is it that we can die but once to save our country." Captain John Montresor, aide-de-camp to British General Howe, reported that Hale's last words were, "I only regret that I have but one life to give for my country."

Eighteen months earlier, Virginia lawyer and legislator Patrick Henry, had made the rafters of Richmond's St. John's Church ring with his impassioned words of defiance, "I know not what course others may take, but as for me, give me liberty or give me death!" To those who knew "Cato," three quotations immediately came to mind: "Chains or conquest; liberty or death"; "Do thou Great Liberty inspire our souls and make our lives in thy possession happy, or our deaths glorious in thy just defense"; and "Gods! can a Roman Senate long debate which of the two to choose, slavery or death?"

But Addison's fame was not made as a playwright, but in collaboration with a college classmate, Richard Steele, as editor and publisher of one of the first newspapers in the English language. Steele had tried his hand at it when he brought out "The Tatler," Addison being one of the main contributors to its columns. Later, Addison took the lead in editing "The Spectator," and, with Steele's assistance, made literary history from March 1711 through December 1714. Through the mouth of his literary creation, Sir Roger de Coverley, the editor poked fun at the foibles and vices of the upper classes of the day, and set a standard for journalists that few have equalled and none excelled.

The Rev. John Wesley, founder of The Methodist Church, was so much pleased with Addison's labors that he said of the newspaper, "The Spectators, written with all the simplicity, elegance and force of the English language, were everywhere read and were the first instruments in the hands of God to check the mighty and growing profanity, and to call men back to religion and decency and common sense." He praised Addison as a man "raised up of God to lash the prevailing vices and ridiculous and profane customs of the country, and to show the excellence of Christianity and Chrisian institutions." What a far cry from the sensational tabloid news-sheets of today!

While a newspaper column is usually the last place one would expect to find a noble Christian hymn printed today, Addison was not the least bit hesitant about printing some of his own original hymns in his paper. In fact, four of his finest appeared in the columns of "The Spectator" within the space of eight weeks in 1712. It was more than a century and a half later that Ira D. Sankey discovered Elizabeth Clephane's poem, "The Ninety and Nine," in an English newspaper, set it to music, and gave the Christian world one of its most effective gospel songs.

The issue of August 23, 1712, carried what Addison called "An essay on the proper means of strengthening and confirming faith in the mind of man." He argued that the Supreme Being makes the best argument for his own existence, the formation of the heavens and the earth being an argument a man of intelligence cannot forbear attending to. Praising the poet, who in Psalm Nineteen (The heavens declare the glory of God and the firmament showeth his handiwork) extols this purpose in exalted strains, he concluded, "As such a bold and sublime manner of thinking furnishes very noble matter for an ode, the reader may see it wrought into the following one." And there followed his majestic metrical version of the Psalm, beginning with these lines:

The spacious firmament on high, and all the blue ethereal sky
And spangled heavens, a shining frame, their Great Original
proclaim.

The last stanza closed with these words:

In reason's ear they all rejoice, and utter forth a glorious voice,
Forever singing as they shine, "The hand that made us is
divine."

While he wrote of Reason as a gateway to God, he himself was a man of great Faith as well as scintillating intellect. Lord Macaulay praised his "cheerful piety" and remarked that "gratitude seems to permeate all his writings."

The day before his death at the age of forty-seven, Addison called his profligate stepson to his bedside and said, "See in what peace a Christian can die." He may well have quoted from another original hymn published in his paper that same year, 1712, that gave "The spacious firmament" to the Christian world, under the caption, "When all thy mercies, O my God," and concluding with these lines:

Through every period of my life, Thy goodness I'll pursue,
And after death, in distant worlds, The glorious theme review.

THERE IS A GREEN HILL FAR AWAY

When playwright John Golden, composer of "Poor Butterfly," a popular song of yesteryear, passed away in 1955, his friends commented on the fact that he had reached the Biblical four-score years prior to his death. Mrs. Frank H. Woodbury, Sr., author of the most famous tear-jerker of the Gay Nineties, "The letter edged in black," went him one better. She died in January, 1953, in a Kansas City nursing home at the age of ninety-one. However, Rev. Charles M. Fillmore beat her record, because this talented Disciples of Christ minister wrote "Tell Mother I'll be there" and many other hymns and gospel songs before his death in Indianapolis in 1952, sometime after he had observed his ninety-second birthday.

But George Cole Stebbins topped them all, even prolific Fanny Crosby who only made it to ninety-five. Had Stebbins lived three-and-a-half months longer than he did, he would have celebrated his one-hundredth birthday. As it was, he left behind him a greater legacy than length of years before he died at the ripe old age of ninety-nine, in Catskill, New York, October 6, 1945. When I read an item in a newspaper in February, 1941, that George Stebbins had celebrated his ninety-fifth birthday, I wrote him a letter, congratulating him on having reached such an advanced age, and thanking him for the hymn tunes he had composed which had meant so much to me. I listed as my favorites from his pen the following, "Take time to be holy," "Saviour, breathe an evening blessing," "I've found a friend," "Out of my bondage, sorrow and night, Jesus I come to Thee," "Have Thine own way, Lord," "Saved by grace," "Jesus is tenderly calling thee home," "In the secret of His presence," and "True-hearted, whole-hearted." To my surprise, a few weeks later, I received a letter from him, dated April 2, 1941, and reading in part, "I am only now able to acknowledge your kind greetings and letter in thanking you for them. . . .

I am still at work disposing of my birthday mail. . . . Thanking you for your kind greeting, I am sincerely and gratefully yours, Geo. C. Stebbins."

The fact that such a distinguished man would take the time and trouble to acknowledge a birthday greeting from someone he had neither met nor heard of, intrigued me, so I sent him a copy of a small booklet containing fifteen of my own original hymns and tunes. Again he wrote that he had received my music and commented at length on my stanzas and hymn tunes. In my files I now cherish three letters in the handwriting of one of the most talented composers of hymns and gospel songs our nation has produced.

Some years later, it was the privilege of our family to visit in the Catskill, New York home where Mr. Stebbins spent his closing years. His niece, who kept house for him in addition to nursing in the local hospital, was very gracious and even permitted me to play on the splendid Chickering upright piano at which Mr. Stebbins had composed most of his finest tunes. Inspired by that visit, we made an extra side trip to Northfield, Massachusetts, where I played and sang "The Ninety And Nine" on the very same organ at which Ira D. Sankey had been seated when he composed the music almost spontaneously in a meeting in Edinburgh, Scotland, in 1874. The organ is in the museum that is housed in the back rooms of what was Dwight L. Moody's Northfield home prior to his death.

In 1878, Stebbins was serving as director of music at Boston's famous Tremont Temple. He had come across Cecil Frances Humphreys' book of poems, "Hymns for little children," and found, among other gems, one entitled, "There is a green hill far away." He learned that the author had written her stanzas in order to explain to a Sunday School class of children the meaning of the phrases of The Apostles' Creed, publishing the volume in Ireland in 1848, the year of her marriage to Rev. William Alexander, and thirty years before they came to the composer's attention. He was delighted with the stanzas and immediately set them to music, making one of the stanzas a chorus. Special services were planned in his Church, with Dr. Pentecost himself doing the preaching, so the musical director

172

decided to introduce his new tune as a male quartet one night that week. Three leading soloists in the city joined with him in learning the new tune, but on the appointed night a very severe storm broke over the city and the three men were prevented from attending the scheduled gathering. As the crowd was unusually small, the service was held in a small lecture room rather than in the main sanctuary, and the composer ventured to sing the new song as a sacred solo. At the close of the service, no one said anything about it one way or the other, so he concluded that it was not as good as he thought it was. Two months later, during another series of evangelistic services when Pentecost and Stebbins were working together in a Church in Providence, Rhode Island, the preacher said, "George, where is that 'Green Hill' you sang in my church?"

Stebbins replied, "The music is my head, but the words I left in Boston." When he found another copy of the stanzas sometime afterward, he said to the minister, "I can sing the 'Green Hill' for you now if you like." The pastor replied, "I wish you would." That time the weather was favorable and the worshippers in a receptive mood, and the song was an instantaneous and inspiring success. The composer later added, "That it was the means of a blessing may be judged from the fact that there were few services when from one to half-a-dozen requests for its repetition were not sent to the platform."

While Stebbins composed and corrected hymn tunes almost to his dying day, few will deny that he had already won for himself an honored place in the life of Christendom with the tunes he had written long before the turn of the century.

WE DEDICATE THIS TEMPLE

"Preaching is in our blood," Ernest Emurian said to his new congregation. "We almost have to preach and sing in our family in self-defense." Following that first service in his new appointment, the Elm Avenue Methodist Church, in Portsmouth, Virginia, the first Sunday in November, 1947, the thirty-five-year-old minister explained his opening statement to some of the Church officers. "My paternal grandfather, Rev. Krikor B. Emurian, was a Protestant minister for over forty years in a little village in Asia Minor where my father was born. A native of Armenia, he lived and labored among his people during a long and fruitful ministry. Mother's grandfather on her mother's side, Rev. Albert G. Rullifson, came over to America from England and founded the famous Bowery Mission in New York City, serving as the first president of its Board of Trustees. Her father, Rev. Harutune Jenanyan, came over from Armenia and studied at Union Seminary, New York, before returning with his Philadelphia bride, to become a pioneer preacher, missionary and educator among his people in Asia Minor. In fact, mother herself was born in a school her father founded, St. Paul's Institute, in Tarsus. Father is an honored Presbyterian minister, while my brother has been, for many years, the Minister of Music in leading Baptist Churches. Around our home we say that all this must make Mother a 'United Brethren.'"

Ernest had been a member of the Virginia Conference of the Methodist Church for eleven years when he, with his wife and baby son, moved from Madison Heights, Virginia to serve the Tidewater congregation. "We fully expected to be going in the opposite direction," Mrs. Emurian told some women of the new congregation. "A Church in Roanoke had sent a committee to see us, and we thought we would be moving west. But, since you can never tell what will happen at a Methodist Conference,

174

we came east instead." The pastor was not too happy about the sudden shift of plans that brought him back to the seaboard section of the Old Dominion, but he and his family entered upon their new work with all the joy and enthusiasm they could muster.

"The building is such a pathetic sight," he told a brother minister, "that it is a disgrace to our denomination as well as to that congregation." The older minister smiled, put his arm around the younger man and said, "Ernest, never judge a Church until you know the people. The Church is not a building, it is a congregation. Learn to love them before you say anything critical about their building."

The new pastor hardly knew what to say, but he resolved to make the best of the opportunity after a happy and progressive ministry of six years in his former charge. His father, Rev. S. K. Emurian, veteran church builder for more than half a century, counselled patience and caution as the son entered upon his new responsibilities. But a brother Methodist advised, "If you can get the place packed to the rafters the first few weeks, they will have to build. So go down there and do it!" The parsonage family moved in the night before Hallowe'en, and when the neighbourhood kids went on their "Trick or Treat" rounds the next night, he turned the tables on them by entertaining them with some sleight-of-hand tricks. As they left, he said, "If you have at least twenty-five kids under twelve at Church Sunday night, I'll show you some more magic." Within four weeks, the night congregations crowded the tiny building to capacity. And, although he had promised his wife and parents that he would "take it easy" that first year, Ernest felt that this was the time to advance. "It is now or never," he said to his people.

The Building Committee met the first week in December, and, in spite of the fact that there was less than thirty-thousand dollars in the building fund, they voted unanimously to proceed with the erection of a spacious new Sanctuary, in accordance with plans that they had been perfecting through the years. When the heavens shook with resounding thunder and the rain began to pour through a leaky roof, one officer said, "I'm not going to vote to spend a penny more patching up that old roof.

Let's put our money on the new Church." In that spirit the people rallied. Ground for the new edifice was broken on Palm Sunday, 1948, and actual construction got under way.

Ernest had been writing hymns off and on for several years, although he had been rebuffed when he went to Princeton Seminary in New Jersey after graduating from the Union Theological Seminary in Richmond, Virginia in 1934. His faculty advisor had looked askance at him when he said, "I want to learn how to write hymns," as if to imply, "Who do you think you are? Ray Palmer or Reginald Heber?" But, undaunted, he had merely postponed his writing for two years. Then one evening, while still a bachelor and residing with his parents in Norfolk, where father and son served adjoining Methodist and Presbyterian parishes, while mother was preparing supper, he sat at the piano and wrote the words and music of a hymn of higher patriotism, "I vow to thee, my conscience." Others had followed, at the rate of one or two a year.

But, during the spring of 1948, as his people were becoming more enthusiastic about their new Church, and rallying to the support of the minister and Church officials, Ernest was inspired to sit down at his desk in the parsonage, located then at 1514 Prentis Avenue, and write a dedicatory hymn for the new Sanctuary. "I plan to write a hymn to be sung to the tune 'Aurelia,'" he said to his wife, Margaret, "and I want to write four stanzas. First, we dedicate the building to God the Father, then to Christ the Son, next to the Holy Spirit, and finally to all three persons in the Trinity." With that in mind, he began to write:

We dedicate this temple, O Father, unto Thee,
The God of ancient ages And ages yet to be;
That here our hearts may worship, And here our songs ascend
In loving adoration And praise that knows no end.

The new hymn was sung at the opening services in the handsome new Church on Easter of 1949 and again when the structure was dedicated free of debt on Easter of 1951. Since then a new parsonage has been built and paid for, an educational annex purchased and equipped and the Church has taken on new life in every department, becoming a vital factor in the religious and cultural life of the city. The pastor was honored by being chosen Portsmouth's "First Citizen" in 1953, in recognition of his contributions to many phases of the city's life.

The new hymn was widely used following its publication in the columns of "The Pulpit," but it did not appear in a major hymnal until "The Hymn Book," prepared jointly by five Presbyterian and Reformed bodies, was published in October, 1955. Meanwhile, the author had written several volumes of religious plays and pageants, as well as dramatizations of hymn stories for Church dramatic guilds and clubs. The third edition of a booklet containing fifteen of his original hymns and tunes was published in 1953. And another hymn, "O God whose voice is in the wind," commissioned for the dedication of the million-dollar Protestant Radio and Television Center, on the campus of Emory University, Georgia, was sung there for the first time in February of 1955.

In his own words, "The providence of God over-ruled our own plans when we came here, but had it not been for these experiences, I probably would never have written what may become my only enduring hymn. If a minister is privileged to write one hymn that is accepted by the Church, his life and ministry are eminently worthwhile."

WE PLOW THE FIELDS AND SCATTER

"Since I have been serving as a Commissioner of Agriculture," forty-two-year-old Matthias Claudius told his friend, Paul Erdmann, "I have often fancied that God is also something of a Commissioner of Agriculture, but on a grander scale."

"You are right," replied Paul. "What is true in the spiritual realm is equally so in the agricultural: Paul plants, Apollos waters, but God gives the increase."

"Would that every farmer in Germany were aware of that fact, Paul," Claudius continued. "Too many of them blame God when their crops fail, and pride themselves on their own personal skills when they enjoy a bountiful harvest."

Appointed one of the Commissioners of Agriculture and Manufacturers of Hesse-Darmstadt in his native Germany in 1776, Claudius had urged the farmers under his jurisdiction to regard their work as a holy task and the rich productive earth as a gift of God. "The clergyman is a steward of souls," he often said, "but you farmers are stewards of the soil. And God needs both to effect a Christian culture and civilization."

During his stay at Darmstadt, Claudius became friendly with the great German man of letters, Goethe, who lived nearby in Frankfurt. He also became acquainted with a group of freethinkers, attending several of their informal gatherings, and listening to their discussions. But, during a severe illness in 1777, he saw the shallow emptiness of their philosophy and became a stauncher and more devout Christian than before.

"The Scripture says, in Psalm Sixty-six, 'Let the people praise thee, O God; let all the people praise thee. Then shall the earth yield her increase; and God, even our own God, shall bless us.' If we give God the praise that is His due, then, and only then, will He give us the knowledge and skill to till the soil so that the earth may yield her increase," he repeated constantly.

Even his writings reflected his new-found Christian fervor

as he seemed to be trying to make up for what he called 'the lost years of his youth.' As a student of law and languages, with a smattering of theology, he served as private secretary to a Danish Count, and had, for a while, been employed on the staff of the Hamburg News Agency. This position enabled him to have some of his poetic works appear in print from time to time, and encouraged him to write more and more when the opportunity presented itself. He soon became so prolific an author that he opened his own publishing house to print his works, and over eight volumes came from his fluent pen between 1775 and 1812. Beside an unusual knowledge of the plays of Shakespeare and the hymns of John Newton, he was a thorough student of the Bible, quoting it whenever the occasion demanded.

"The Bible says, 'The earth is the Lord's and the fulness thereof, the world and they that dwell therein,'" he often reminded his listeners. "Furthermore, we are told in Holy Writ that 'Every beast of the forest is mine, saith the Lord; and the cattle upon a thousand hills; I know all the fowls of the mountains and the wild beasts of the field are mine.' The very rain that comes down from heaven is a gift of God." He affirmed this conviction over and over again. "Does not the Bible say, 'Thou waterest the ridges thereof abundantly; thou settlest the furrows thereof; thou makest it soft with showers; thou blessest the springing thereof. Thou crownest the year with thy goodness and thy paths drop fatness?' The Psalmist is constantly telling us 'He sendeth His springs into the valleys which run among the hills. He watereth the hills from His chambers, and the earth is satisfied with the fruit of thy works. He causeth the grass to grow for the cattle; the herb for the service of man, that he may bring forth food out of the earth.'" And he would close by asking the Biblical question, "'What shall I render unto the Lord for all His benefits toward us?'" To which there was but one answer, personal dedication.

It was at a feast held in the home of Paul and Anna Erdmann that Claudius was inspired to write one of his finest poems. The simple and humble things of life furnished him the inspiration he needed to express his deepest feelings. Seeing the moon rising in the heavens one night in 1779 as he walked down a footpath leading by the river side at Darmstadt, he had composed his beautiful poem, "The fair moon hath ascended." Now, three years later, watching the children playing games together, as their parents conversed over the topics of the day, seeing the tables laden down with all kinds of bounties from nearby fields and farms, and fully conscious of the deep-rooted religious heritage that had undergirded his people for generations, he turned to his host and said, "All good things around us, Are sent from heaven above. Then thank the Lord, O thank the Lord, For all His love."

"We must, Matthias, and we will," Paul had replied. "The very jollity of our children is almost a reverent act of gratitude to God for His abundant blessings and His measureless mercies."

"It is so refreshing to escape from the sham of city life and the intrigues of politics," Paul added, "and mingle once again with real God-fearing people, whose lives are built on genuine spiritual foundations, and who can truly be said to enjoy life in the finest and fullest sense of the word."

"We have our failings, Matthias," Paul said, "but underneath it all, our people possess a strong and vital religious faith and a freedom to express it in so many different ways, thanks to the boldness and faith of Martin Luther."

During the next few days, that fall of 1782, Claudius was haunted by the memories of the delightful harvest festival he had attended. He could not get away from the majesty as well as the utter simplicity of it all. Under the spell of those memories, he began to write a poem, which, translated by Jane Campbell, opened with these lines:

We plow the fields and scatter The good seed on the land,
But it is fed and watered By God's Almighty hand.
He sends the snow in winter, The warmth to swell the grain,
The breezes and the sunshine, And soft refreshing rain.

His three stanzas bore out the truth he preached wherever he went: "God is the creator of all things, the giver of our daily bread. The only thing we can give Him in return is 'our humble, thankful hearts.' "

While originally intended as a song for school children, this harvest festival poem has now found a lasting place in Christian hymnody. Although the author lived thirty-three years after he wrote it, he never produced another that was its equal. And of all the poets of what is sometimes called 'The golden age of German literature' he alone enjoys the distinction of having produced a poem that is worthy of being sung universally as a noble Christian hymn.

WHERE CROSS THE CROWDED
WAYS OF LIFE

"But I am not a hymn writer, Professor," Dr. Frank Mason North protested. "A Methodist minister, yes; but not a writer of hymns," he continued. "Why don't you try your hand at it yourself?" he asked his friend, Caleb T. Winchester, Professor of English Literature at Connecticut's Wesleyan University. "You didn't do too badly with the hymn you wrote for the dedication of the Judd Hall of Natural Science at your Alma Mater."

"You know about that?" his friend asked.

"Why not? Nearly everybody else does. You wrote 'The Lord our God alone is strong' in 1871 and it was included in the Methodist Hymnal of 1878," Dr. North replied.

"Well, let me put it this way, Doctor," the Professor explained. "Years ago Lowell Mason coaxed Ray Palmer to produce a new hymn, until the young man showed him a poem entitled 'My faith looks up to Thee,' which he had written during his private devotions two years earlier. Now, I do not claim to be a Lowell Mason, nor am I here to coax you to show me a hymn you have already written for some previous occasion. I made the trip here from Middletown, Connecticut, as a member of the Commission which has been charged with the responsibility of preparing a new Methodist Hymnal, to ask you to seriously consider writing a new hymn for this forthcoming volume. In your position as Corresponding Secretary of the New York Missionary and Church Extension Society, you are just the man to undertake this responsibility."

Dr. North looked out of the window of his office in the Methodist Headquarters, New York City, and saw part of the teeming throngs that crowded the streets of the world's largest city. "Hasn't Washington Gladden already done what you are asking me to do?" he asked. "His hymn, 'O Master let me walk with Thee' develops the theme you have suggested. As a hymn of Christian service, it is unexcelled."

"If Gladden could do it in Columbus, you can do it in New York," Winchester replied.

"But Gladden is a poet at heart, and I am not," North protested.

"He did not consider himself a hymn writer either," the Professor stated, "and he was the one who was most surprised when Dr. Charles Richards took his poem which he found in the 'Sunday Magazine' the year Gladden wrote it, and made a hymn out of it. Yet this hymn, which he wrote in 1879, and the equally famous poem, 'Behold a sower from afar,' which he wrote in 1897, have won for themselves a lasting place in Christian hymnody."

"Are you suggesting that anything I write may be fortunate enough to enjoy the same fate?"

"Why not? Stranger things have happened in Church history as you yourself know only too well. Incidentally, if Rev. James Freeman Clarke had not pressed Julia Ward Howe to write worthy stanzas for the music of 'Glory, glory, hallelujah,' she would not have given to the world 'The Battle Hymn of the Republic.' So if I feel like a combination of Mason and Clarke, you will have to understand my position and do your best under the circumstances," he continued, as he rose, reached for his hat and coat, and extended his hand to Dr. North.

"I'll do what I can," North promised, as he and his friend said their 'Goodbyes' and the visitor left. That afternoon, in 1903, Dr. North looked back upon a long and fruitful life of fifty-three years. A native of the great metropolis, he had graduated from Wesleyan University and served several Methodist Churches in different states before taking up the duties that now occupied all of his time and energy. He had been laboring in and around New York City since 1892 and if anyone knew the struggles of city life, he was the man.

"If anyone is qualified to write a hymn about the city's need of Christ, North is the man," Winchester had informed the committee, whereupon the other members had commissioned him to make the personal contact and do what he could to produce the hymn.

The next few days were very busy ones for the Secretary and it was near the end of the week before he resumed preparing a sermon that had been on his heart for some time. Picking up the Bible, he read again the Lord's parable of the Marriage Feast found in the twenty-second chapter of Matthew. When he came to the ninth verse, he paused and read the words over several times, "Go ye therefore into the highways and as many as ye shall find, bid to the marriage." Accustomed to reading his texts in several translations, to get new insights into the meaning of Jesus' words, he picked up the American Revised Version, and discovered that the word translated "highways" in the Authorized Version of 1611 was rendered "parting of the highways" in the more recent volume. In his mind's eye he pictured the strategic crossroads of history and the famous squares where important streets converged in the great cities of the world. "Those crossroads are always crowded with people," he said to himself, "yet Christ is there too, if they only knew it. Like Cleopas and his companion on the road to Emmaus, they cannot see that He is walking by their side." Before he realized it, Frank Mason North was writing a poem on the theme suggested by the sermon. The first stanza contained these moving lines:

Where cross the crowded ways of life, Where sound the cries
    of race and clan,
Above the noise of selfish strife, We hear Thy voice, O Son of
    Man.

In the Methodist Hymnal of 1905, this hymn appeared for the first time as a hymn, although previously published as a poem in "The Christian City" of which the author was editor.

Later, for the centennial celebration of Drew Theological Seminary in 1917, he wrote "Thou Lord of light, across the years." That same year he penned "The world's astir! The clouds of storm" for the Children's Day celebrations of the Methodist Church, after an appeal for such a hymn from Dr. Abram W. Harris. In 1928, seven years before his death, at the request of Dr. Henry H. Meyer for a "world service" hymn, he wrote "O master of the waking world." So to Winchester, Harris and Meyer all Christendom is indebted for drawing from the fertile brain and fervent soul of this renowned clergyman three of the outstanding hymns of the twentieth century. Of the numerous honors heaped in great profusion upon this distinguished leader, none can surpass the tribute paid him by the ecumenical Church which accepted and is now using with profound effect the hymns he wrote during his long and eventful life.